PRACTICAL

FENG SHUI
SOLUTIONS

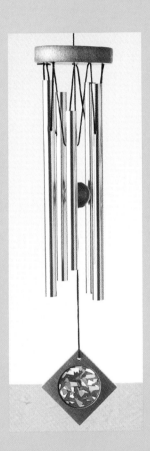

SIMON BROWN

CASSELL&CO

First published in the United Kingdom in 2000 by
Cassell & Co
Wellington House
125 Strand
London WC2R 0BB

First published in 2000
Reprinted 2000

Created and produced by Carroll & Brown Ltd
20 Lonsdale Road
London NW6 6RD

Project Editor: Madeleine Jennings
Senior Designer and Illustrator: Sandra Brooke
Photographers: David Murray, Jules Selmes

Text © Simon Brown 2000
Design and layout © Carroll & Brown 2000

Distributed in the United States of America by Sterling Publishing Co., Inc.
387 Park Avenue South, New York, NY 10016-8810
A CIP catalogue record for this book is available from the British Library.

ISBN 0 304 35476 7

Reproduced by Colourscan, Singapore
Printed and bound in England by Butler and Tanner Ltd

contents

how to use this book

The basic principle of Feng Shui is that the life force flowing through your surroundings, known as chi energy, has a profound influence on the way you think and feel. The layout, orientation and contents of your environment all affect the flow of chi, which explains why you may have noticed that certain places or atmospheres are much more conducive to your success than others. The aim of Feng Shui is to help you make simple, positive changes to the arrangement and decor of your home or workplace. This, in turn, helps to alter the flow of chi energy in such a way as to promote your health, wealth and happiness.

This book is a collection of over 100 Feng Shui answers to commonly experienced problems, ranging from how to meet the right partner or be a better parent, being more successful in your career or finding ways of increasing your wealth, to overcoming ill health. Each solution is in fact a collection of several different ways to change the atmosphere or chi energy of your home, almost all of which are simple and inexpensive. For example, many problems can be resolved simply by moving your bed from one area of your bedroom to another. You can also effect changes by including a particular colour, pattern or shape into the decor.

Other solutions are more complicated and involve making a scale drawing of your home to determine which areas of your home or office fall in which compass directions. This is because many of the solutions depend on placing an item or changing the decor in a particular compass direction of your house or apartment. For example, you may be advised to place a yellow flowering pot in the south-west of your home if you wish to deepen friendships, keep two red roses in the west to feel more romantic, or situate a metal pendulum clock in the north-west to help make a smooth transition from working to retirement. Instructions on how to make an accurate Feng Shui floor plan of your home or office are provided on pages 8-10.

To put the solutions I offer in this book into practice, it is not necessary to have a complete understanding of Feng Shui. However, if you are interested in finding out more, special pages on 'The Principles of Feng Shui' – chi energy, yin and yang, Five Elements, Eight Directions and Nine Ki astrology – appear in the first two chapters of the book. Throughout the remaining chapters there are special pages that explain the powerful and recurring 'Tools of Feng Shui' – plants, flowers, mirrors, crystals, avoiding electromagnetic fields, water features, iron, sea salt, sounds, patterns and shapes, colours, building materials, dimensions and lighting – that can also be used to stimulate helpful chi energies and protect against harmful ones. If you

A deep understanding of Feng Shui is not required to use this book but, if you so desire, there are pages that explain its principles and tools.

CHAPTER ONE covers health issues, such as diet and nutrition, fitness, pregnancy, general ailments, emotional well-being and sleeping problems.

CHAPTER TWO consists of problems relating to wealth, such as how to improve your wealth, maintain your wealth and change your attitude to money.

CHAPTER THREE covers relationship issues, such as finding a suitable partner, ensuring commitment, resolving sexual problems or ending a relationship amicably.

CHAPTER FOUR contains solutions to family issues, such as problems with mealtimes, children, relatives, celebrations and family dilemmas.

CHAPTER FIVE concentrates on matters relating to your career, for example, how to find employment, ensure success, resolve general problems and deal with retirement.

would like to read more about any of these, the contents list will direct you to the relevant pages. To learn about Feng Shui in greater depth, I recommend that you read my other books: *Practical Feng Shui*, *Practical Feng Shui for Business* and *Practical Feng Shui Astrology*.

HOW TO USE THIS BOOK

This book is divided into five chapters, each relating to a general aspect of life. To solve a particular problem you may have, decide which of the five chapter headings it falls under – health, wealth, relationships, family and career. Next, turn to the beginning of that chapter where you will find a further list of topics. Specific questions relating to these topics can then be found on the relevant pages. Read through the questions until you find the one that most closely resembles your own dilemma.

For example, if you have been dating for a while and still haven't managed to meet someone who interests you, turn to the relationship chapter opener on page 65. You will see that there are five further headings: friendships, finding an ideal partner, ensuring commitment, resolving sexual problems and resolving general problems. As you read through the questions listed under the second heading, you will see one that addresses this specific problem: 'I have been single for some time. Although I meet people, I have not been able to find the right person. Please give me some Feng Shui suggestions'. If you cannot find listed the exact problem you are facing, find the question that is most similar and implement those remedies instead. Sometimes you will need to pinpoint the root cause of a problem particularly carefully. For example, if you feel you are not generating as much wealth as you think you should be, your predicament may stem from a lack of financial awareness, an inability to save money, or an unhelpful attitude to money – all of which are covered in Chapter 2. While the solutions to any of the questions listed under one of these topics may help to a certain extent, you will get the best results if you identify the question that relates most closely to your problem.

Once you have found the relevant question, read through all the recommendations I have given. Start with the easiest one; sometimes this will be sufficient to resolve your problem. At other times you may have to implement several of the solutions I recommend before you notice an improvement. If you cannot find a question that deals with your dilemma, you can still use the principles of Feng Shui to work out a solution. For example, if you are unhappy, you can identify whether it would help to be more yin or yang. You can then decide which of the chi energies of the Eight Directions would be most beneficial and which Nine Ki phase would be most auspicious for you.

At the end of many solutions, I have included the best times to make the necessary changes in life. This advice is based on the Eastern system of astrology, known as Nine Ki. In order to put this into practice, you need to identify your 'Nine Ki year number', which is based on your year of birth. For more details, see pages 52–3.

Depending on the Feng Shui solution I offer, you will find that the pages in this book are generally illustrated in one of four ways shown right.

When the solution is to introduce a specific chi energy into a space, a textured panel appears behind the text with a photograph to illustrate the type of atmosphere you need to create.

When the chi energy of many directions can be enhanced or calmed, a small compass is shown. A section of this is highlighted with items to place in that direction of your home.

When the solution is to enhance or calm the chi energy of one specific direction, most of the page is illustrated by one direction, accompanied by objects and items to place there.

When the solution involves rebalancing your personal chi energy, the pages have illustrations that show you how to absorb more yin or more yang chi energy.

You will also find that I have listed solutions that have little to do with changing the atmosphere in your home, but concentrate on eating certain types of foods or adopting a healthier lifestyle. These are found under the heading 'Just common sense'. Other features that you will find on some pages include the clearly labelled 'Things to avoid' box.

It may take a few weeks before you see some improvements or results, so be patient and remember that Feng Shui is not a magic pill – it should be seen only as a tool to help you deal with problems in life and should in no way supersede any medical or other professional advice you receive.

In my opinion, the greatest benefit of Feng Shui is that it helps you to be more aware of your environment and the impact it has on feeling in control of your life. Much of our unhappiness results from feeling that a situation is unchangeable. Yet, we can cope with all kinds of difficulties if we somehow feel it is within our power to effect changes. Feng Shui is one such way of being able to feel in control of your destiny and my experience of Feng Shui over the last ten years has been a testimony to this. Although it has not stopped me from experiencing problems, Feng Shui has made it much easier to deal with them because I feel that their resolutions are ultimately within my power.

I do not believe, however, that Feng Shui is the only or best way to achieve this: a macrobiotic diet, exercise and positive thinking have all played important parts in my life at different stages. Just as other people have been instrumental in getting me through difficult times, Feng Shui is only one piece of the jigsaw puzzle.

making a floor plan

To apply the Feng Shui solutions that I have provided in this book, you need to know which parts of your home are influenced by which types of chi energies. This involves finding out which rooms are falling in which direction and then assessing the quality of chi energy related to that direction (see pages 40–1). To do this you will first need to make an accurate floor plan of your home. When I refer to 'your home' this is the space you live in, irrespective of whether you own it or rent it. If you live in an apartment, with a shared entrance and other shared facilities, you should concentrate on the parts that are for your sole use. If you live in a flatshare, work with the whole flat.

Your floor plan needs to be accurate and to scale, so drawing it onto graph paper will help. If your home has two floors draw separate plans for each floor. The first step is to use a long tape measure and measure the length and width of each room in your home. These measurements then need to be converted into a convenient scale, for example, 1 metre equals 1 centimetre, or 1 foot equals ⅛ of an inch, then use a ruler and pencil to draw each room in its appropriate position onto paper.

Next, add the features of your home onto the plan. These should include doors, windows, alcoves, fireplaces, stairs, large beams, steps and any outdoor water features such as a pond,

To draw up floor plans you will need a compass with an outer rotating dial (available in camping or hiking shops), a tape measure, a ruler, pencil and paper, preferable graph paper.

fountain or swimming pool. You do not need to measure their size, but try to draw them in proportion to each of the rooms. Make sure you indicate on your floor plan which way the doors open into a room.

Home fixtures and furniture are important in Feng Shui so these also need to be added onto your floor plan. Include the stove, kitchen sink, fitted cupboards, bath, shower, toilet, aquarium, beds, chairs, desk, kitchen table and dining table.

FINDING THE CENTRE OF YOUR HOME

Once you have drawn your basic floor plan, the next task is to find the centre of your home. If your home is a rectangle, square, circle or octagonal shape, then this should be simple: draw diagonal lines between opposing corners or opposite points on a circle, and where they intersect is the centre. These shapes are also considered favourable in Feng Shui.

More complicated is an irregular-shaped home, such as an L-shape. The geometric method for finding the centre of these shapes is to break the area down into two rectangles. Draw diagonal lines between the opposing corners to get the centre of each rectangle, then draw a line between the centres of each rectangle. On another piece of transparent paper, break the L-shape into two opposite rectangles and draw a line

Draw each floor of your home and divide it up into rooms and hallways. Measure the dimensions and convert these so that your floor plan will be to scale. Find the centre by drawing lines from opposite corners. Where they cross is the centre.

Find magnetic north by aligning the floor plan with your home, using the front door or a wall as reference. Use a compass to locate magnetic north, then draw a line from the centre of your floor plan outwards to magnetic north.

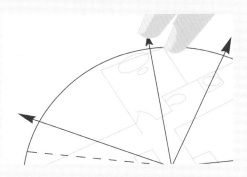

Trace the Eight Directions from page 10 onto transparent paper, then cut this out and place it on top of your floor plan. Align the centre points and the lines showing magnetic north. Now you can see which rooms fall in which directions.

between their centres. Place the transparent piece of paper over the first and where the two lines cross is the centre of the whole space.

An easier way to find the centre of a complicated-shaped home is to stick the floor plan onto a piece of thick card and cut the card out to the shape of your home. Hold the card horizontally and try to find its point of balance on a long pin. Once the card is balancing on the pin, pierce the card. The hole will mark the centre of your home.

If you can't find the balancing point of an L-shaped home, it may be because its centre is actually outside the shape. Stick a thin piece of paper between the wings of the L-shaped building where the centre is likely to be. This gives you something to balance the pin on, but it won't affect finding the centre of the shape. Alternatively, you can attach a piece of cord to one corner of the floor plan you have cut out, hang the card by the cord and draw along the path of the cord. Repeat this from one other corner and the point at which the lines cross will be the centre.

ALIGNING THE GRID OF THE EIGHT DIRECTIONS

Once you have found the centre of your home, you need to find magnetic north. To do this, you will need to use a compass. Place your floor plan on a flat, horizontal, non-magnetic surface so the walls of your floor plan are aligning with the same walls of the room you are in. Place the compass over the floor plan with its centre aligning with the centre of the floor plan. Turn the compass around until the needle lines up to north, then mark this on your floor plan and draw a line to the centre.

Next, trace or photocopy the grid of the Eight Directions (see below) onto transparent paper, then cut around it so the directional lines extend to the edge of it. Make sure you line the centre of the grid to the centre of your floor plan and the north of the grid to the north that is marked on your plan. Mark off the segments of the Eight Directions onto your floor plan and draw lines between those points and

the centre. Now you will know which parts of your home lie in which directions. There are a number of things that can distort a compass reading, such as concealed iron or steel beams, pipes, water tanks and electrical appliances. For this reason I always take a compass reading in several areas of a building, including outside of the building, until I am sure I have a consistent reading.

Many schools of Feng Shui divide the grid of Eight Directions into equal wedges of 45 degrees, but the Japanese compass style I use divides it into four segments of 30 degrees and four segments of 60 degrees. Note that magnetic north is marked at the bottom in Eastern maps.

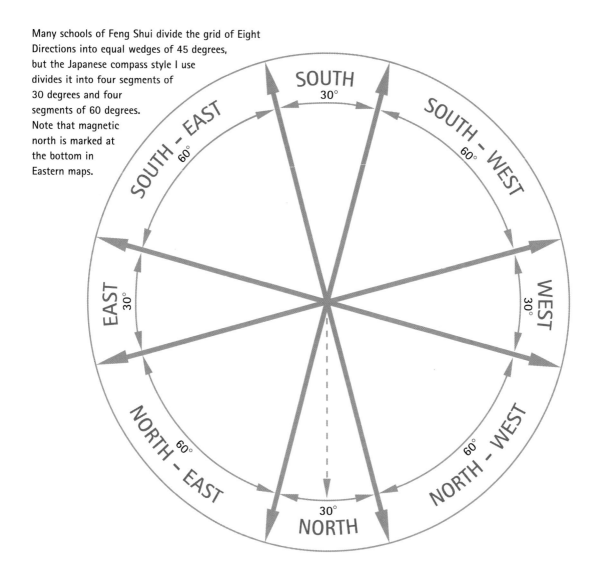

HEALTH

1

problem

I know I eat too much junk food and not enough healthy foods, but it is a difficult habit to break. How can I start eating a more balanced diet?

just common sense

Instead of trying to alter your eating habits overnight, include healthy foods to your meals gradually. For example, include a vegetable and a healthy grain, such as brown rice, barley, couscous, pasta or wholegrain bread, in each meal.

solution

Like any changes to your lifestyle, you need to be motivated by a good reason. Among other things, a healthy diet will increase your fitness, improve your appearance and foster general good health. Whatever your particular reason for cutting down on junk food, keeping pictures of yourself in good health around the home, particularly the kitchen, will serve as a visual reminder of your goals and help you stay focused when you are tempted to give up.

To encourage you to eat more healthy foods, create an atmosphere in your home where junk food seems out of place. You can do this by decreasing the presence of artificial chi energy in your home, while increasing the presence of natural chi energy. To promote healthy, natural chi energy, fill your home with items made from natural materials, such as wooden furniture. Plants and fresh flowers will also refresh chi energy, as will fresh air and sunlight, so draw back curtains and open windows whenever possible. A moving water feature in the east or south-east of your home also adds healthy, natural chi energy.

To decrease the artificial energy that is associated with processed foods, reduce the amount of electrical equipment you keep in your house, particularly microwave ovens. Similarly, synthetic carpets, plastic objects and furniture made from MDF (medium density fibreboard) will create a more artificial atmosphere that further removes you from nature and natural foods, so avoid these where possible.

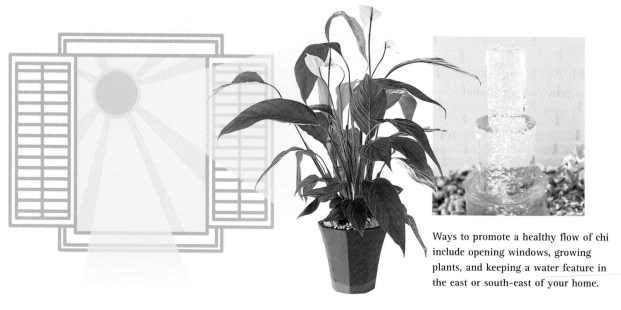

Ways to promote a healthy flow of chi include opening windows, growing plants, and keeping a water feature in the east or south-east of your home.

problem

I suffer from strong chocolate cravings and frequently eat chocolate between meals. I am determined to give it up and would appreciate some advice.

solution

To reduce the temptation to eat between meals, organize yourself so that you eat your main meals at exactly the same time each day. Your digestive system will then develop into a rhythm where it will know when to expect a meal and, providing the meals are well balanced, nutritious and satisfying, your need to snack between these times will diminish.

Fostering the chi energy of the north-west will help you feel more organized and better able to set up a routine. To absorb more north-western chi energy while you sleep, position your bed so that the top of your head is pointing north-west. To increase this chi energy in your home, place a pendulum clock made with as many metal parts as possible in the north-west of your home. The pendulum will set up a rhythm to the flow of north-western chi energy and the metal will help to regulate the flow. An alternative to the clock would be a heavy metal paper weight or any other object that is heavy and made of metal. Keeping your home neat, clean and tidy will also encourage you to be more organized and routine-based.

If you still feel the need to snack, wean yourself off chocolate by eating healthy alternatives such as fresh fruit and raw vegetables instead. Raisins and roasted nuts are good substitutes because the raisins provide that similar sweet taste, while the nuts have that rich, roasted quality found in chocolate. Bread and hummus or rice cakes with sugar-free jam are other good alternatives.

If you have associated eating chocolate with rewarding yourself, try to develop a similar emotional connection to your alternative snacks as this will make the substitution easier. You can do this by eating your healthier snacks in a happy and positive environment, such as your favourite room, or while playing your favourite music.

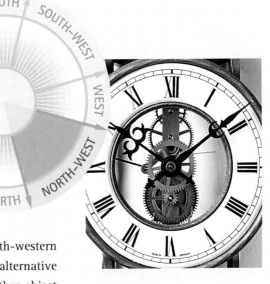

A metal pendulum clock or any other heavy metal object placed in the north-west of your home will help you to stop snacking between meals.

problem

I am desperate to lose weight, but every time I diet I give up soon after starting. Sometimes I even put on more weight than I had before. How can Feng Shui help me?

If your kitchen is clean and tidy, with a pleasant and relaxing ambience, you are more likely to spend time preparing healthy meals there. Play your favourite music while you cook and keep fresh flowers on the table.

solution

Changing your habits, especially the foods you eat, is not easy. If you can find a sensible and realistic diet that encourages you to lose weight gradually, you will be more inclined to stick to it and maintain your ideal weight. As for Feng Shui solutions, the chi energy of the north-west encourages greater self-discipline, while the chi energy of the south-east fosters persistence and tenacity. Building up these energies in your home and increasing your exposure to them will therefore improve your resolve to stay on a diet.

In Eastern medicine, the north-east and south-west relate to the stomach and pancreas, and the west and north-west relate to the large intestine. Keeping these directions of your home clean, tidy and free from clutter will enable positive chi energy to flow more freely. Healthy plants in these areas will further increase the amount of beneficial chi energy surrounding you.

To develop greater enthusiasm for your lifestyle change, try sleeping with the top of your head pointing south-east or east. Sleeping with the top of your head pointing north-west will enhance the energy related to greater discipline, which will also help you stick to your diet.

To make cooking and eating healthier foods as pleasurable as possible, make your surroundings attractive so you will want to spend time there. Keep the kitchen clean and tidy and play your favourite music while you cook. Placing fresh flowers on the dining table and using attractive crockery will make the eating process more relaxing and will therefore encourage your aims.

just
common sense

The biggest factor in losing weight is reducing your intake of saturated fats. Replace meat, dairy foods and processed foods with grains, seafoods, vegetables and fresh fruit. Minimizing your intake of sugar, artificial sweeteners and fried foods will also help to cut down the calories and encourage weight loss.

solution

To improve your daughter's eating habits, you need to ensure that all aspects of her life are as positive and balanced as possible. If she is too yang, she will feel tense and physically unable to eat very much, whereas if she is too yin, she may suffer from low self-esteem, which could inhibit her appetite.

To build up your daughter's yang chi energy, and therefore help her to be less sensitive and inward-looking, encourage her to play sports and generally be more physically active. Try to make sure that she isn't eating too much sugar, as this can lead to swings in blood sugar levels and strong cravings for nutritionally empty foods. Meals high in complex carbohydrates – such as pasta, brown rice, couscous, polenta, barley and porridge – and vegetables and beans, will help her to maintain more stable blood sugar levels. Also, the more varied her diet, the more she will relax, which will in turn boost her appetite.

If you think your daughter's poor appetite stems from low self-esteem, she would benefit from being exposed to more eastern chi energy. To achieve this, turn her bed so that the top of her head points east when she sleeps. Plenty of plants and bright green-coloured objects in her bedroom, and a moving water feature in the east of your home will further increase her exposure to eastern chi energy.

If mealtimes have become embattled and you need to strengthen the positive aspects of your relationship with your daughter, try to enhance south-western chi, as this relates to motherhood and family relationships. To do this, place yellow flowers or pieces of charcoal in a clay container in the south-west of your home. Alternatively, keep sea salt in ramekin dishes in the north-east and south-west.

According to the principles of Eastern medicine, eating and digestion are associated with the skin. Your daughter may therefore be able to stimulate her appetite by scrubbing her skin every day with a hot, damp cotton towel. This will improve her circulation, help her skin to breathe and promote a generally healthier appearance.

By strengthening your relationship with your daughter, you will have a better chance of encouraging her to eat well. This can be achieved by placing some charcoal in a clay dish in the south-west of your home.

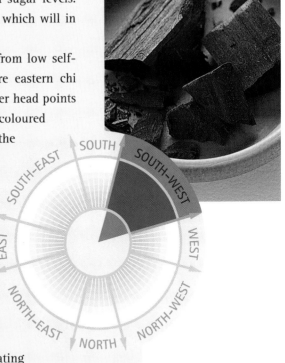

chi energy

Feng Shui is based on the principle of a subtle electromagnetic force called chi energy. It flows around the human body and throughout the universe carried by wind, water, light, sound and the sun's energy. In fact, the Chinese characters for Feng Shui mean 'wind' and 'water', reflecting the way chi energy moves. The chi energy that you are exposed to influences your thoughts, emotions and health. By placing yourself in a position where the surrounding chi is most favourable to your aims, you can achieve goals more easily and effectively. This is the primary aim of Feng Shui.

PERSONAL CHI

Chi energy flows around your body carrying your thoughts, ideas and emotions in a similar way to blood transporting oxygen and nutrients around your body. When you are feeling happy and positive, the chi energy circulating around your body is vital and healthy. When you are feeling depressed or sad, the flow of chi energy is slow, dispersed and unhealthy. If your feelings or thoughts change, your body's cells will be fed with a different kind of chi energy. However, you can also change your personal chi energy by exercising, eating different kinds of foods and living and working in different environments. In this way, chi energy operates as a two-way process: the way you

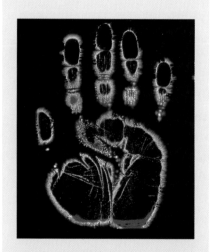

Personal chi extends up to 1m outside the body, so it is influenced by other people's chi energy and the chi energy of your immediate environment.

think influences your chi energy, and the chi energy that circulates around your body causes you to think or feel in a certain way.

You can manipulate your personal chi energy to effect the changes you desire. When you are feeling angry, for example, this is a sign that your chi energy is too concentrated and intense. If you breathe slowly and deeply while stretching your limbs, your chi energy will slow down and spread around your body. Manipulating personal chi energy in this way is one of the solutions I often advocate to help people overcome their problems.

Your personal chi energy does not stay inside your body: it typically extends between 10cm and 1m around your body. This means that your personal chi energy field can be easily influenced by other types of chi energy. The foods you eat, the clothes you wear, the weather and the people with whom you interact can all influence your personal chi energy. In Feng Shui terms, however, the primary influence is the chi energy of your surroundings, be it the home, the office or outdoors.

CHI ENERGY IN BUILDINGS

All buildings have their own chi flowing about that mixes with and influences your personal chi energy. High ceilings allow chi energy to move vertically, especially if there are skylights or tall windows. An atmosphere with this kind of energy helps you to feel more objective, original and independent, and I often get my best ideas when I'm in a cathedral, museum or large hall. Rooms that have low ceilings make it easier for chi energy to move horizontally, especially if there are windows or doors facing each other on either side. The horizontal movement of chi fosters interaction and sociability, and I enjoy being in these kinds of spaces when I want to spend time getting to know someone better.

A room or building with one large entrance, a domed roof or a round floor plan causes chi energy to become concentrated, which is good for focusing your energy or gathering up your strength. I use these spaces if I need to accomplish something or finish a difficult project. A room with many windows and doors will disperse chi energy more easily, particularly if the windows go down to the floor and the building is at the top of a hill or mountain. I find this ideal when I need to contemplate the bigger issues in life.

UNFAVOURABLE CHI

Many problems in life are due to blocked or inauspicious chi, and many of the solutions that I provide in this book are in fact ways to correct this.

Chi energy that flows quickly in a straight line will make it harder to feel settled and could contribute to health problems and emotional imbalance in the long term. This is most likely to occur when there are several doors in a line along a long corridor or when your stairs lead directly to the front door of your home.

Chi energy that flows too slowly can lead to stagnant chi energy. If you are surrounded by this chi, it is more likely that you will feel depressed and lonely. Stagnant chi energy is most likely to occur in homes where there is little natural light, such as basement flats and homes that face north.

stagnant chi

OVERFURNISHED ROOMS consisting of heavy curtains, tapestries, rugs, cushions and other soft fabrics will generate a slower flow of chi energy. Slow-moving chi can often turn into stagnant chi energy, which can make you feel depressed, isolated and lonely. To remedy this chi, get rid of the soft furnishings and keep lots of healthy plants in the room.

cutting chi

PROTRUDING CORNERS that jut out into a room can cause fast-moving, cutting chi energy. This type of chi can disorientate anyone sitting or sleeping in that room. To remedy cutting chi, place a bushy plant in front of the corner. This helps to slow and soften the flow of chi energy.

problem

I know how important regular exercise is, but I never seem to be able to stick to a regime for any length of time. I would be grateful for any help Feng Shui can offer.

solution

Even where they do exercise, many people find they lack the necessary will power to keep going after their initial enthusiasm has worn off. A few changes to your home and exercise clothes can help you to feel more motivated and energetic.

A spacious atmosphere is not only healthier, it can also help to inspire you to keep fit. A home that is overfurnished with soft chairs, cushions, carpets and curtains will produce an atmosphere that encourages you to feel lethargic and unmotivated. Keeping your home reasonably empty, and growing as many indoor plants as practical, will create a lively, fresh ambience.

To feel more motivated and competitive, paint your walls white and leave them uncluttered. Walls that are beige, brown, pink, dark maroon or grey will be less stimulating, particularly if they are used to display paintings and pictures. If your home has small rooms with low ceilings, you will find it a greater challenge to turn it into an energetic and stimulating environment than if it has large, tall rooms. In these small rooms, up-lights will create the impression that the ceilings are higher.

To align yourself with a more energizing type of energy, try sleeping with the top of your head pointing east, south-east, south or north-east. If you are a light sleeper, opt for the south-east as the other directions can be too stimulating for deep sleep.

The material and colour of the clothes you wear during exercise will influence your personal chi energy. To ensure your body and chi energy breathe properly, make sure your garments are of pure cotton. Synthetic fibres can upset your flow of chi energy. To help keep your energy levels high, choose an active, stimulating colour. White, red, yellow, fiery purple and orange will all have an invigorating influence on your chi energy.

solution

Feeling tired and sluggish is a sign that you are too yin. To adjust the balance, you need to surround yourself in a more yang environment and eat foods that contain more yang energy.

To make the atmosphere in your home more yang, decorate with bright colours, particularly reds, yellows and oranges. Keeping surfaces clear and living spaces free from clutter will allow chi energy to move about faster and so generate more yang energy. Hanging more mirrors and keeping plants with pointed leaves will also encourage a faster flow of chi, making your home feel more active. As an additional measure, try playing rhythmic music on your sound system: the vibrations it emits will stimulate your senses and make you feel more dynamic.

Yang foods that will increase your energy levels include complex carbohydrates. These release energy slowly but enduringly, which is why they are good for beating lethargy, as opposed to 'quick hit' sugary foods. It will be easier to absorb complex carbohydrates if you chew your food well (at least thirty times per mouthful). Root vegetables, beans, nuts, seeds and fish are also yang.

Physical exercise is a great way to boost vitality, if you can only find the energy to get going! You may feel more motivated if you display pictures around your home of yourself or other people playing sports. Another way to maintain your enthusiasm is to keep a timetable of your exercise routine or a record of your physical performance in a prominent place where you will regularly catch sight of it.

To feel more active and alert, try moving your bed so that the top of your head points eastward when you are sleeping.

To feel more dynamic and alert, try absorbing more yang energy. You can do this by eating complex carbohydrates, such as rice, displaying shiny mirrors in your home and listening to or playing rhythmic music.

problem

My partner and I both lead unhealthy lifestyles: I overdo the cigarettes, while he drinks too much. How can we give up these bad habits?

just
common sense

You may have developed your habits in association with another activity, for example, having a cigarette with a cup of coffee or pouring yourself an alcoholic drink when you come home from work. By going to the gym straight after work and steering clear of coffee, you will avoid falling into the pattern of behaviour that leads you to drink or smoke.

solution

One way of solving this problem is to change your attitudes: instead of seeing it as giving up a pleasurable pastime, substitute drinking and smoking with another enjoyable activity, for example, a sport or hobby. This way, neither of you will feel as if you are denying yourselves.

As for Feng Shui solutions to your problem, if you feel you need to deepen your resolve to give up your unhealthy habits, it would help to become more yang. This can be achieved by wearing bright-coloured clothing, undertaking physical sports, spending more leisure time outdoors and eating more hot meals. Decorating your home with glass or stone sculptures and metal or hardwood furniture will surround you in a more yang environment.

If you feel your dependence on cigarettes and alcohol is due to stress and tension, you should aim to become more yin. This can be achieved by doing gentle stretching exercises and meditation, or by receiving a massage. Pale green, light blue and cream are relaxing yin colours, so wearing clothes or choosing fabrics for your home in these colours will also help. Plants with large floppy leaves will radiate more calming yin energy, as will soft furnishings and rugs.

To be more self-disciplined and better organized to carry out your resolution, sleep with the top of your head pointing north-west. To feel more motivated, sleep so the top of your head is pointing north-east.

To encourage your efforts and avoid a relapse, display visual reminders of your goals. These could include holiday snaps of you and your partner looking fit and happy or doing a physical sport.

A yin lifestyle that includes a relaxing hobby can prevent you from turning to cigarettes and alcohol when stressed. Becoming more yang by playing outdoor sports and decorating your home with bright colours and stone objects will make you more determined to give up these bad habits.

solution

Even though you and your partner might be in perfectly good health, it can take several months before you conceive, so try not to worry if you do not succeed immediately. In Feng Shui terms, the chi energy of the north is most helpful for conception. To expose yourself to more northern chi energy, sleep in such a way that the top of your head points northward. Alternatively, try to have your bed in the north of your bedroom or home.

You can also increase the presence of northern chi energy in your home by decorating it with cream colours. Pure cotton cream bed linen will generate more northern chi energy and you will be surrounded in it while you sleep. Cream-coloured walls will reflect the optimal light frequencies back into the room, helping to calm your chi energy in a way that is more receptive to becoming pregnant.

Placing a mirror or crystal in the northern part of your home will also activate northern chi energy and increase your chance of conceiving. Wear pure cotton clothing as this will prevent exposure to the static electricity generated from synthetic materials, such as nylon and rayon, which is considered bad Feng Shui.

A year when your Nine Ki year number is in the north will be the time when your chi energy is most conducive to conception. Other auspicious times to become pregnant are when your Nine Ki year number is in the north-east or west.

problem

We have been trying to conceive for a while without success. Can I improve our chances using Feng Shui?

just
common sense

You are more likely to conceive when you and your partner are in good health, so try to eliminate the stresses in your life and ensure that you get enough sleep. Maintain a diet that is high in grains and vegetables, and cut down on saturated fats, sugar, alcohol and acidic foods, such as coffee, wine and tomatoes. These are thought to reduce a man's sperm count.

NORTH

problem

I am pregnant and would like to know what, if anything, I can do to make my pregnancy go as smoothly as possible.

solution

The emotions of a mother-to-be generate a chi energy that not only circulates through her own body, but also through her baby's. This means that a mother's health and emotional well-being are of vital importance to her unborn child. To ensure beneficial chi energy both to yourself and to your baby, you need to feel content, secure and relaxed. Having a bright and clean home will help you feel happy and make it easier to feed your unborn baby with beneficial thoughts.

To encourage positive emotions, arrange pictures and photographs around your home that make you smile. You should also listen to your favourite music and watch videos that make you laugh. To calm the flow of chi energy around your home, use lots of rugs, large cushions and fabrics. Pale greens, blues and creams are relaxing colours, so try to decorate with these where possible. Ornaments that have curved, flowing shapes will also add quiet chi energy to a space, helping you feel serene and restful.

To add healthy chi energy to your space, grow plenty of green leafy plants there. Not only will these help to clean the air, the very act of looking after them is harmonious with the chi energy required for nurturing a developing baby.

The south-west is associated with motherhood so try to ensure that this part of your home in particular is clean and tidy. To boost the chi energy related to nurturing, place a yellow flowering plant in a clay container in the south-west of your home. If you feel frustrated and unsettled during your pregnancy, try sleeping with the top of your head pointing south-west for a while.

Your unborn baby may be vulnerable to the high intensity electromagnetic fields that are emitted from electrical equipment. While you are pregnant, therefore, it's a good idea to keep at a safe distance from computers, televisions, microwaves, photocopiers, hairdryers, electric fan heaters and electric blankets.

You will feel most comfortable being pregnant when your Nine Ki energy is in the north, south-west or west direction.

One Feng Shui remedy to this problem would be to keep a yellow flowering plant, such as this ranunculus, in the south-west of your home.

solution

Until you actually experience it, it's hard to predict how you will feel and what you will want during labour. What's more, because your needs may change during the different stages of childbirth, it's best to have as many options as possible. You may want to have clear, open spaces to move about in or a more cosy environment made up of large cushions, bean bags and blankets. You may wish to squat, lean forward or hang from something, in which case, a low stool, the back of a tall chair or a window ledge will all be useful. To keep your options open, prepare a few rooms in different ways.

If your labour occurs at night, you may find the artificial light distracting. To create a more yin, diffused and calming atmosphere, switch off bright overhead lights in favour of more indirect lighting that is reflected off a wall or ceiling. Low lights with lampshades can create a more settled ambience, while candles radiate the softest light of all, creating the ideal atmosphere for your baby's first introduction to the world. Surrounding yourself with colours and visual images that make you feel happy will also reflect different light frequencies into your peripheral chi energy field and positively alter the way you feel.

To help you stay calm, play music while you give birth. The sound waves will relax your superficial chi energy, helping you to stay calm and will also distract you from the pain. A foot and ankle massage, with particular attention paid to your little toes and the areas above your ankles on the inside of your leg, will stimulate the acupressure points that can ease labour pains.

To encourage bonding, prepare your bedroom so that it makes you feel content and restful. The bed should be comfortable, the lighting low, and fabrics natural and in muted colours. Remove any electrical equipment as this could generate electromagnetic fields that can be disturbing to your baby.

problem

I am going to have a baby soon and am planning a home birth. What can I do to ensure that the delivery goes well and to provide a welcoming environment for my baby?

yin and yang

There are two kinds of chi energy: the more passive yin energy and the more active yang energy. These relative terms are used to compare all things in the universe, be they personalities, emotions, thoughts, careers, leisure activities, diets or homes. Everything is either more yin or yang depending on what they are compared to. For example, resting is considered more yin than working, but more yang than sleeping. The goal behind the concept of yin and yang is to make it easier to be successful in life. If you need to be more yin to accomplish something, such as being more romantic, then you would aim to surround yourself with more yin influences. If you feel you would succeed by being more yang, for example, being more assertive, then using yang influences to make your chi energy field more yang would help.

The concept of yin and yang is useful in Feng Shui because it helps you to understand how you interact with your environment. An imbalance of yin and yang may be the cause of problems you are experiencing, so if you can diagnose whether you are too yin or yang, you can change aspects of your environment to help you redress the balance.

The chart on the right will help you to decide whether you are more yin or yang. Because yin and yang are relative, it is easiest to judge when you compare yourself to other people.

more yin

IF YOU SUFFER FROM ANY OF THESE PHYSICAL OR EMOTIONAL AILMENTS, YOU ARE PROBABLY TOO YIN:

depression, insecurity, loneliness, worry, pessimism, helplessness, lethargy, feeling cold, infectious illness, diarrhoea

IF YOU WANT TO FEEL MORE OF THE FOLLOWING, YOU WILL NEED TO BE MORE YIN:

relaxed, calm, imaginative, creative, artistic, sensitive, caring, receptive, supple

more yang

IF YOU SUFFER FROM ANY OF THESE PHYSICAL OR EMOTIONAL AILMENTS, YOU ARE PROBABLY TOO YANG:

aggression, violence, tension, frustration, anger, impatience, ruthlessness, cold-heartedness, stiffness, constipation, high blood pressure, dry mouth, dry skin, frequent minor accidents

IF YOU WANT TO FEEL MORE OF THE FOLLOWING, YOU WILL NEED TO BE MORE YANG:

alert, quick, focused, precise, accurate, confident, determined, physically strong

PLANTS with large or round leaves are more yin, as are curved ornaments, mottled patterns, irregular lines, rag-rolling, coarse brushing, plaster finishes and pastel colours like blue and pink.

TABLECLOTHS and napkins create a more yin atmosphere, as will soft furnishings, such as bean bags, large floor cushions and sofas. Thick carpets, rugs and full-length curtains also have more yin energy.

TABLE LAMPS with cream, beige or yellow cloth shades, and indirect lighting that is reflected off the wall or ceiling will create a more yin environment. So too will candles, closed doors and peaceful, relaxing music.

FLOORING made from wood, tiles or stone introduces more yang energy into your home, as do clutter-free, open spaces, bright, direct halogen lighting and formal-looking furniture.

SHINY METAL OBJECTS in your home will create more yang energy there. Polished surfaces, mirrors, wooden blinds instead of curtains, white walls and ceilings, and a real fireplace will also do this.

FLOWERS and other bright yellow, red, orange or purple decorative objects generate more yang energy in your home. So too will spiky plants and playing music that has a distinct, rhythmic beat.

problem

Since moving to this home several years ago, I have been experiencing steadily increasing headaches. Can Feng Shui remedy the situation?

solution

Headaches can result from extremes of being either too yin or too yang. If your headaches occur when you are under stress and feeling irritable, then it is likely that you are too yang. A yang headache is usually concentrated at the back of your head and in your neck. It may also be accompanied by stiff and painful shoulders. A yin headache is often located around the front of your head, especially your forehead, and feels similar to a hangover.

If you are prone to yang headaches, the solution is to become more yin. To surround yourself in a more yin atmosphere, decorate your home with calming colours such as pale green, light blue or cream. Curved shapes, mottled paint finishes, soft surfaces, flowing fabrics and indirect or low lighting all add soothing and slow-moving chi energy to your home. Place bushy plants in front of sharp protruding corners and tall plants under any beams in your house. Sleeping for a while with the top of your head pointing north will immerse you in the quieter and more yin water chi energy.

A diet filled with fresh vegetables and fruit will also make you more yin. Yoga, t'ai chi and meditation are all activities that relax you and help to prevent headaches caused by stress. If you want someone to relax you instead, try shiatsu massage, aromatherapy or reiki.

If your headaches are more yin, you need to surround yourself in a more dynamic, yang atmosphere. This can be achieved by giving your home a spring clean: wash curtains, shampoo carpets and throw out any clutter. Discourage damp or stagnant energy by opening windows and allowing more fresh air to flow through your home. Whenever you start to feel sluggish, take a brisk walk.

Eating more salty, alkaline yang foods and consuming less sugary, acidic foods, alcohol and chocolate will also discourage yin headaches. Miso soup, sauerkraut and pickled plums (umeboshi) are all helpful yang foods.

If your headaches are at the front of your head, surround yourself in more yang energy by eating soups and other warming foods. Opening the windows to let in fresh air will also help. If your headaches are at the back of your head, immerse yourself in more yin energy by having indirect lighting at home and pursuing relaxing hobbies.

solution

According to Feng Shui philosophy, heavy, stagnant or sticky chi energy encourages asthma. Therefore, if you are an asthma sufferer, the ideal atmosphere to have in your home is one where the air is clean, fresh and free from dust, and there is no dampness or mildew.

Dust is most likely to collect in rugs, carpets, curtains and soft furnishings so, if possible, opt for wooden floors and blinds instead. If you cannot do this, make sure you wash and air fabrics and covers frequently. Plants absorb moisture and help to keep the air clean, so keep plenty in the home, particularly in the kitchen and bathroom where dampness and mildew can build up. Growing plants in your bedroom will also radiate good chi energy while you sleep.

The west and north-west are the directions associated with your lungs, so try to ensure that these areas of your home in particular are clean, tidy and dust-free. To prevent chi from stagnating in these areas, avoid having rubbish, rotting foods or wilting flowers there. If you move again in the future, avoid homes where the kitchen, bathroom and utility rooms are in the west and north-west, and make sure that each room has a window.

The well-being of your skin will also subtly affect your lungs, so always wear clothes made from pure cotton or other natural fabrics – synthetic materials carry a charge of static electricity that can irritate your skin. Scrubbing with a hot, damp cotton hand towel every day will also help to refresh and invigorate your skin.

problem

My asthma has become significantly worse since moving to my new home. How can Feng Shui help?

things to avoid

Avoid foods that make the blood more sticky, such as dairy foods, eggs and meat. Processed grains such as bread, pasta and noodles may aggravate asthma, so substitute them with wholegrains such as brown rice, barley and oats. You should also include leafy green vegetables in your diet as they can increase the chi energy of your lungs.

problem

I have suffered from rheumatoid arthritis for some time, but since I retired and moved home, it has become worse. What would help to relieve this problem?

solution

In Feng Shui, the condition of the bones and joints relates to water chi energy. Damp conditions, a diet high in water chi energy or an inability to expel water chi energy from your body, therefore, will aggravate rheumatoid arthritis. Increasing the presence of tree chi energy in your home will drain away excess water chi energy and help to solve the problem. Decreasing your exposure to metal chi energy, which can otherwise encourage water energy, will also help.

To add more tree chi energy to your home, decorate with the colour green. To absorb humidity, grow lots of leafy plants, especially in the north of your home. Wooden furniture, surfaces and floors all help to keep the atmosphere dry and reduce the risk of creating an environment that has too much water chi energy. If you have a fireplace, light it often. Candles will further help, as long as you continue to build up tree chi energy in your home.

To absorb more tree chi energy, sleep with the top of your head pointing east or south-east. A bed with a wooden base, cotton wadding mattress (such as a futon), and pure cotton sheets will also immerse you in more tree chi energy while you sleep.

Because metal chi energy can increase the presence of water chi energy, avoid having metal objects and surfaces in your home. Similarly, reduce the amount of grey and silver you use around the home as these are colours that are associated with metal chi energy.

Wine, coffee, sugary drinks, cold drinks, ice cream and an excess of fruit can all create too much water chi energy in your body. To soak up this excess, eat foods that are associated with tree chi energy, such as leafy greens, leeks, spring onions, radishes, mooli and sauerkraut.

solution

According to Eastern medicine, the occasional cold is seen as a useful way to exercise your immune system, clear out toxins and force you to have a rest. If this happens too often, however, it is a sign that you are becoming too run down and weak.

Being surrounded in a more yin, cold and damp environment increases the risk of catching a cold. To create a atmosphere of general dryness and warmth, light candles or a natural fire, or turn on the central heating. Whenever there is a dry sunny day, hang your bedding outside to air it and allow it to soak up the sun's warming yang rays. To make sure there is space for energy and air to circulate easily, open the windows every day and try to keep your home relatively free from clutter. This will encourage a more yang environment.

Plants are useful for absorbing moisture, so keep plenty of these in your home, especially in the kitchen and bathroom. They will also keep the air clean, fresh and healthy.

Strong, bright colours will also help to create a more yang and warming atmosphere in your home. Yellow or orange walls will make a room feel warmer, but you can also place yellow, orange or red decorative objects around the house to achieve this brightening effect.

To make yourself more yang, eat warming soups, stews or casseroles that contain grains and root vegetables. You should also reduce the amount of sugary foods you eat. Exercise, body scrubs and rising early in the morning will further help you to become more yang.

Absorbing more warming, yang energy will help to prevent you from catching colds. To do this, soak up the sun's rays and eat hot stews and soups. Plants absorb excess moisture, so grow plenty in your home, especially in the bathroom and kitchen.

problem

Since moving to this home, I have been catching a lot of colds. What are the Feng Shui solutions to this problem?

things to avoid

Make sure there is no dampness in your house; quickly wipe up any spillage in the kitchen and bathroom, don't leave water in the sinks, fix any leaking taps and remedy any rising damp. Objects that have mildew growing on them, such as shower curtains, should be thrown away.

five elements

Refining the principles of yin and yang further, chi energy can be broken down into five types: tree, fire, soil, metal and water chi energy. Called the Five Elements, they are related to the seasons (spring, summer, late summer, autumn and winter respectively) and certain times of the day. The five times of day are morning, midday, afternoon, evening and night. By imagining the atmospheres of these times, you will be able to get a feel for the kind of chi energy related to each element.

THE FIVE ELEMENTS CYCLE

Just as the seasons and times change cyclically, the five types of chi energy relate to each other in a cycle as well. The unique way in which the Five Elements relate to one another is a fundamental principle of Feng Shui and a useful tool when implementing the Feng Shui solutions that I recommend in this book.

Each element supports or enhances the energy of the following element. For example, water supports tree, which supports fire, which supports soil, which supports metal, which, completing the cycle, supports water. As it does so, it loses some of its own chi energy, but this is replenished by the preceding chi energy.

If one of the Five Element chi energies becomes deficient, the preceding chi energy will jump

across and have a destructive influence on the following element. For example, if tree chi energy is deficient, water will have a destructive influence on fire chi energy. Ideally, there should be a good balance of all the Five Element energies in your home, so aim to have at least one item from each of the lists opposite in every room.

USING THE FIVE ELEMENTS TO SOLVE PROBLEMS

Each of the Five Elements is associated with a range of emotions, which are listed on the chart opposite. By manipulating the relative strengths of the elements, you can therefore exercise a certain level of control over your emotional life.

If you feel dominated by a negative emotion, consult the chart opposite to find out which element it relates to. Next, you should try to reduce the presence in your life of the chi energy associated with that element by strengthening the chi energy of the following element in the cycle. You should also aim to strengthen the preceding element to avoid a destructive relationship with the other elements. To take an example, depression is associated with metal chi energy. If you are feeling particularly low, you may be able to lift your spirits by increasing the presence of soil and water chi energy in your surroundings, in the ways listed in the chart opposite.

Each element supports its proceeding and preceding elements, but has a destructive effect on the two remaining elements in the cycle.

tree

FEELINGS RELATED TO THE FIVE ELEMENT TREE: anger, impatience, frustration, hastiness, carelessness

PLANTS, especially tall ones, add more tree energy to a room, as do wooden objects or surfaces; green colours; tall items, such as coat stands; up-lights; and vertical striped patterns.

fire

FEELINGS RELATED TO THE FIVE ELEMENT FIRE: hysteria, melodrama, excitability quarrelsomeness

LIT CANDLES or fireplaces; bright lights; sunlight; bright red or purple; pointed, star shapes; triangular, pyramid shapes; zigzag patterns; and plants with pointed leaves all add fire energy to a room.

soil

FEELINGS RELATED TO THE FIVE ELEMENT SOIL: dependency, cautiousness, slowness, indecision, jealousy

CLAY, TERRACOTTA, and other earthenware objects; yellow, brown or beige colours; low-spreading plants in clay containers; low, wide furniture, such as coffee tables; and rugs, carpets and curtains all add soil energy to a room.

metal

FEELINGS RELATED TO THE FIVE ELEMENT METAL: depression, introversion, indecision, pessimism, sensitivity

STAINLESS STEEL, iron, brass or other metal objects; hard stone surfaces such as slate, granite or marble; white, grey or silver colours; and round, spherical or dome shapes all add metal energy to a room.

water

FEELINGS RELATED TO THE FIVE ELEMENT WATER: anxiety, fearfulness, irresponsibility, loneliness, isolation

GLASS TABLE TOPS; glossy black or translucent cream colours; mirrors and glass-fronted pictures; wavy lines and mottled patterns; curvy furniture; and creeping plants all add water energy to a room.

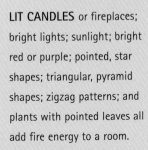

problem

I am trying to adopt a more positive attitude to life. I have read lots of self-help books on the subject, but I am interested to see if Feng Shui can promote this aim.

solution

The chi energy associated with being positive is similar to the kind of energy that occurs when the sun rises, and is therefore found in the east, south-east and south of your home. To absorb more of the energies of these directions, move your bed so that the top of your head is pointing in one of these directions when you sleep.

If you have a choice of entrances to your home, use one that is to the east, south-east or south of the centre of your home as this will encourage more positive chi energy to enter your home. If your front door or front windows face one of these directions, your home will already contain plenty of this energy.

Bright colours such as green, red and purple radiate positive energy, so choose clothes, bed linen, curtains, frames and other furnishings and decorative objects in these colours to surround yourself in more of this energy. Remember, the brighter the colour, the more powerful the influence. Bright green will be most effective in the east, south-east and south of your home, whereas reddish purple will work best in the south, south-west and north-east.

Placing a water feature in the east of your home will increase the chi energy associated with feeling confident, self-assured and capable of making things happen – attributes that cannot but help you to have a positive outlook on life!

You may find that being slightly more yang will help you with your aims, so try to incorporate more yang foods in your diet. Eat more grains and hot vegetables, and less cold meals, sugary foods and soft drinks. To make your home more yang, keep rooms well aired and clutter-free. Pointy-leaved plants generate more yang chi energy, as do bright colours and hard, clear surfaces.

It will be easiest to adopt a positive attitude when your Nine Ki year number is in the east, south-east or south.

Using an entrance that is to the east, south-east or south of your home will encourage positive chi to enter it. Bright greens, reds and purples also generate positive chi, so furnish and decorate your home in these colours.

solution

Sunlight is very important for making us feel cheerful, particularly in winter when there is less of it about. During these months, not only do we lack the biological stimulation that results from exposure to sunlight, but the cold atmosphere also affects our mental outlook. To compensate for a lack of sunlight, one of the best solutions is to use a real fireplace. If you have a real fireplace, light it regularly. If you don't, light candles when you are at home, particularly in the north-east part of your home or room.

To create a warmer atmosphere, introduce to your home bright colours, such as reds, oranges and yellows, by way of pictures, cushions and fresh flowers. Choose pictures that make you feel positive about the future. Up-lights reflected off the ceiling can help create a more uplifting atmosphere, as this tends to stimulate a more upward flow of energy. A brightly lit ceiling is also more similar to a sunny sky, rather than lights directed onto the floor.

To align yourself with a more sunny and upbeat energy while you sleep, try sleeping with the top of your head pointing east, south-east or south, particularly as you find you get depressed easily.

To prevent the debilitating effects that cold and dampness can have on your environment and personal chi energy, keep the atmosphere of your home dry. Soft furnishings, curtains and carpets are particularly vulnerable to damp. Make sure you have an effective heating system and use any dry, sunny winter days to air fabrics outside. On these days, it would also be helpful to open up the doors and windows and give your home a thorough clean.

To cope with the cold and damp, make yourself slightly more yang by eating more warming dishes such as thick soups and stews, and grains, such as porridge. Eating fewer sugary foods, salads and raw fruits will also make you more yang, as will doing vigorous outdoor sports and activities.

problem

I moved into a dark and damp home a few years ago and have since felt depressed. My depression is particularly acute during the winter. Do you have any advice?

problem

Lately, I have been very irritable and find myself snapping at other people readily. I generally feel tense, especially when at home. How can Feng Shui make a difference?

Eating lots of fruit will help you to become more yin and content, as will furnishing your home with curvy-shaped chairs and fabric lampshades.

solution

Being cranky and short-tempered is a sign that you are too yang. To feel more content and at ease, you need to become more yin, which can be achieved by immersing yourself in a more yin environment.

To slow the flow of chi energy and create a more relaxed, yin ambience, keep lots of pale green, light blue and cream decorative objects in your home. Fabrics and soft furnishings in these colours will also help, as will low or indirect lighting. Lights reflected off a wall or ceiling and table lights with lampshades will help to create a softer atmosphere in the evening.

Curved shapes, textured surfaces and mottled, wavy or irregular patterns will further slow the flow of chi energy, so try to incorporate these features into your home. Plants with rounded or floppy leaves have a calming effect, so grow lots of these in your home as well, especially in front of any protruding corners or along long corridors.

To absorb more relaxing chi energy when you sleep, turn your bed so the top of your head is pointing south-west, west, north-west or north. You should also face one of these directions when you are sitting in the living or dining room.

Eating lots of fruit, salads and vegetables will boost your personal yin energy. Similarly, wearing soft, flowing and pastel-coloured clothing will encourage you to feel more at peace.

It will be easier to feel calm when your Nine Ki year number is in the north, south-west, west or north-west.

things
to avoid

Sharp, protruding corners; long, straight corridors; too many shiny objects; and mirrors that face each other, a door or a window. These will all speed up the flow of chi energy in your home and make you feel tense.

solution

In Feng Shui terms, jealousy is primarily associated with the soil chi energy of the south-west and, to a lesser extent, the soil chi energies of the centre and north-east. To overcome your preoccupation, you should therefore aim to calm these energies and reduce your exposure to them.

To subdue the chi energy of the south-west, centre and north-east, place small ramekin dishes filled with one or two tablespoons of sea salt in the south-west and north-east areas of your home. Sea salt is extremely yang and absorbs chi energy, which will help to stabilize the flow of soil chi energy. If there is a door, staircase, bathroom, toilet or kitchen in one of these directions, the potential for jealous feelings increases, so make sure you place the sea salt on the floor next to any doors, at the foot of any stairs or anywhere in one of these rooms. Placing metal pots, paper weights, clocks or any other heavy metal objects in the south-west, centre or north-east of your home will also help to calm the offending soil chi energy, as will decorating with white, grey and silver objects in these areas.

Healthy plants radiate a positive chi that will encourage the right kind of atmosphere for you to discuss your insecurities with your friends. Keeping as many plants as possible in the south-west, centre, and north-east of your home, will therefore help you to work through your jealous feelings to a more beneficial outcome.

To build up your confidence and make you feel less insecure, sleep with the top of your head pointing east or south-east.

It will be more difficult to overcome jealous feelings when your Nine Ki year number is in the north-east or south-east.

problem

I tend to be a rather jealous person and am constantly preoccupied with whether my friends pay too much attention to other people. How can Feng Shui help me with this problem?

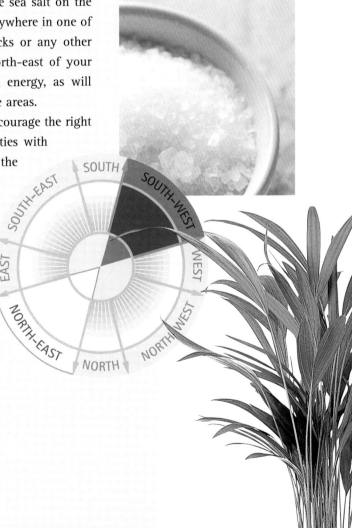

Growing healthy plants and placing ramekin dishes filled with sea salt in the south-west and north-east of your home will help to calm the chi energies that relate to jealousy.

problem

I often live in the past and dwell on previous negative experiences. Obviously this is affecting my everyday life and I would like to move on. How can Feng Shui help?

solution

According to Eastern medicine, past experiences are related to your back. The meridians or pathways of chi energy that run along this part of the body are associated with the water chi energy of the north. The contracted metal chi energies of the west and north-west also make it harder for you to let go of the past. To move forward with your life, you therefore need to minimize the presence of these energies in your home and increase those of the east and north-east.

To start with, undertake a major spring clean in the the north, west and north-west of your home. By keeping these areas clean and tidy, you will discourage a build-up of chi energy that makes it hard for you to let go of the past. If your bathroom, toilet or kitchen are in any of these directions, keep them well aired and dry because any dampness or mildew increases the risk of chi energy stagnating.

The chi energy of the north-east is helpful for clearing your head of the past, changing direction and motivating yourself to move ahead. To increase this energy in your home, decorate the north-east with white flowers, objects made of stone or white rocks.

Eastern chi energy increases your enthusiasm for focusing on the future. Wooden furniture and objects bring out this energy, so incorporate wood into your home wherever possible. Light-coloured wood is better than heavy, dark wood. To further enhance eastern chi energy, keep a bowl of fresh, clean water in the east of your home. Brilliant whites, greens, blues and purples also encourage you to move on, so have as many of these colours as possible in your home.

To reduce metal and water chi energy, avoid having lots of metal and glass surfaces and objects in your home. Similarly, avoid decorating your home with off-white, grey, silver, black, brown or cream colours.

Your efforts to forget about the past and move forward will be best rewarded when your Nine Ki year number is in the east, south-east, south or north-east. It will be more difficult to achieve your aims when your Nine Ki year number is in the north, west or north-west.

Increasing the presence of eastern chi will give you the enthusiasm to focus on the future. To boost this energy, keep a bowl of fresh water in this direction of your home.

solution

Overexposure to northern chi energy can make you worry more than normal, as will being too yin. The Feng Shui solution, therefore, is to reduce your exposure to northern chi energy and make yourself more yang. Increasing the presence of eastern, south-eastern, southern, north-western and north-eastern chi energy in your home will all help by boosting your overall confidence in different ways.

If there is a door in the quieter northern part of your home, you can increase the amount of yang energy it generates by painting it red, attaching a shiny metal door handle or hanging a metal wind chime in front of it. Alternatively, surround the door in as much red as possible by attaching red flowers or ribbons to it, or by having a red doormat.

If there is a bathroom, toilet, utility room or kitchen in the northern part of your home, try to ensure it contains furniture and surfaces made from wood, wicker or bamboo – all these materials help to calm the detrimental northern chi energy. Tree energy, particularly in the form of plants, also has the distinct advantage of draining the water chi energy associated with the north and rooms with water-related functions.

As rooms in the north are unlikely to receive direct sunlight, there is a greater risk of chi stagnation. By keeping plants in these areas, you will encourage the flow of healthy chi energy. Ivy is a good option because it requires little light. If there is insufficient light, you may need to experiment with a daylight bulb to encourage the plants' healthy growth.

Glass, marble, granite and stone are all yang materials, so have furniture and decorative objects made from these in your home. Follow a more yang diet, concentrating on fish, grains and root vegetables, and cut down on sweets, raw fruits, iced drinks, coffee, wine and sugary soft drinks, which are all comparatively yin. Martial arts and vigorous outdoor exercise will also help you to become more yang.

I get very anxious about little things and this often prevents me from taking on new challenges. How can I change this behaviour and become more courageous?

Becoming more yang will make you less likely to worry. To absorb more of this chi energy, take up an outdoor sport and eat more yang foods. Plants in the north of your home, especially bathrooms, will also help.

problem

Since starting a new relationship, I find it hard to make decisions or do anything by myself. How can I change this and become more independent?

solution

In Feng Shui, being too dependent can be due to an excess of the settled, south-western soil chi energy. Too much of this energy can make it harder for you to strike out on your own. To achieve greater independence, you therefore need to reduce your exposure to south-western soil chi energy. The chi energy of the north relates to independence, so immersing yourself in more of this energy will also help to solve this problem.

To calm the detrimental south-western chi energy, place a ramekin dish or any other small, round white china bowl filled with one or two tablespoons of sea salt in the south-west of your home. Putting heavy metal objects, such as a metal statue, in this part of your home will also calm this energy. If you have a door or staircase in the south-west of your home, this chi energy will move around your home very freely. To slow it down, place bushy plants close to the door and by the stairs.

To feel more decisive generally, expose yourself to more north-western chi energy by hanging a metal pendulum clock in the north-west of your home. Its rhythmic tick will encourage you to organize yourself. Decorating this direction with off-white, grey and silver colours will also increase your exposure to this helpful energy.

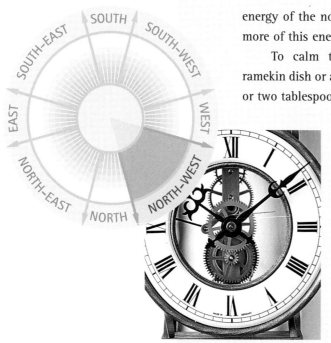

One way to become more organized and decisive is to keep a metal clock, preferably with a pendulum, in the north-west of your home.

To gain more self-confidence, surround yourself in eastern chi energy by putting a water feature in the eastern part of your home. Becoming more yang can also help you become more confident and decisive, so undertake some form of physical exercise and eat more yang foods such as fish, grains and root vegetables.

To feel more in control of your life, reposition your bed so that you sleep with the top of your head pointing north-west. You should avoid sleeping with your head pointing south-west.

If your Nine Ki year number is in the south-west, your efforts to become more independent may not be very successful. If this is the case, you should try undertaking these solutions in the following year when your Nine Ki year number is in the eastern phase.

solution

In Feng Shui terms, mood swings are aggravated by unstable environments that cause your personal chi energy to change too quickly. Typical features in your home that can create an unstable flow of chi energy include stairs that lead to the main entrance, long corridors and a few doors in a straight line. To counter the effects of these, I recommend that you grow lots of leafy green plants around these areas. Hanging up thick, fabric curtains or putting down rugs on the floors in these parts of your house will also regulate the flow of chi energy.

When you are feeling depressed, you can adjust your own chi energy by spending more time in big, open spaces or in rooms with bright colours and hard surfaces. To adjust your chi energy so that you don't feel overactive, try spending more time in comfortable, cosy places that have plenty of soft furnishings.

One way to create greater stability in your life is to develop daily routines that you stick to. For example, try to eat your meals at exactly the same time each day and go to bed at the same time every night. By doing this, your body will build up a rhythm that will help to moderate any mood swings. To help bring a routine into your life, sleep with the top of your head pointing north-west, the direction associated with gaining greater stability and self-discipline. A metal pendulum clock placed in the north-west of your home will also encourage you to develop a routine.

If your Nine Ki year number is in the south or centre, you may find it harder to control your moods.

problem

I suffer from extreme mood swings. One moment I feel very happy and the next I could be plunged into a deep depression. Do you have any suggestions that would help make me feel more balanced?

Having a more balanced personal chi energy will make you less prone to mood swings. If you are feeling overactive and more yang, sit in a comfortable chair. If you are feeling depressed and more yin, surround yourself with and wear bright colours.

things
to avoid

Sugar can affect your moods almost instantaneously. Refined sugar or similar sweeteners are rapidly absorbed into the blood stream, giving you an instantaneous 'high'. To reduce blood sugar levels, your pancreas secretes insulin, which often results in lowering your blood sugar levels even further, making you feel tired and depressed. This creates a vicious cycle as you start craving sugar to pick you up again. Reduce your intake of sugar and try to eat more complex carbohydrates instead.

PRINCIPLES OF FENG SHUI

eight directions

In Feng Shui, there are eight key directions, each with a distinct kind of energy. By familiarizing yourself with the characteristics of these directions and energies, you have another tool to help you overcome problem areas in your life. For example, the chi energy of the south is associated with sociability, so if you are feeling introverted you can expose yourself to more southern chi energy.

Each direction is associated with a number of features that combine to provide its unique energy. These features are a time of day, season, symbol from nature, Five Element, colour, Nine Ki number, a family member in a traditional Eastern family, and a trigram. A trigram is a series of three parallel lines that are either broken or solid. A broken line represents yin and a solid line represents yang. There is also a chi energy of the centre of a room or space – where all the Eight Directions meet – but it has no associated trigram, symbol, family member, time of day or season.

The easiest way to build up one of these energies is to move your bed so that the top of your head is pointing in that direction when you sleep. This is because outside chi energy enters your body most easily through the crown of your head. You can also sit facing one of these directions, for example, when you are at your desk at work.

To find out which areas of your home or office are facing in which direction, and are therefore affected by specific energies, you will need to draw up a floor plan of your home (see pages 8–10).

SOUTH-EAST

4

Mid morning
Spring changing to summer
Wind
Eldest daughter

The wind symbol makes this chi energy excellent for spreading ideas, so it is a good energy to absorb more of if you want to boost communication skills, be it through talking, writing, film, art or music. It is a creative and imaginative kind of energy, and is helpful for making progress in life, particularly progress that is related to future prosperity.

EAST

3

Morning
Spring
Thunder
Eldest Son

Representing the new day, this energy is ideal for starting new things, like a business, career or job. Its upward-flowing nature encourages confidence, enthusiasm and ambition. The symbol of thunder gives it a louder, forceful edge which is helpful for going out and making things happen. It is a helpful direction to sleep in if you want to wake up and get up earlier.

NORTH-EAST

8

Early morning
Winter changing to spring
Mountain
Youngest son

This piercing and quick-changing energy is good for clearing your mind, being more decisive and thinking of new directions to take in life. It also encourages you to be more competitive, work harder and spot new opportunities, particularly the chance to make money.

SOUTH

9

Midday
Midsummer
Fire
Middle daughter

This fiery, passionate chi energy is useful for self-expression, encouraging you to be warm-hearted, sociable and generous. It is also a good energy for promoting yourself, winning awards and gaining public recognition.

SOUTH-WEST

2

Afternoon
Summer changing to autumn
Earth
Mother

An ideal energy for improving the quality of your work and being more practical and realistic. The settling soil energy helps to deepen relationships – be they with friends, lovers or family. As it is associated with the mother, it also encourages caring feelings, particularly with your family.

CENTRE
5

The chi energy of the centre links all the Eight Directions and is the most powerful of all chi energies. It does not have a specific trigram, time or season but can be said to represent them all. As such, it is an energy that can help you become the centre of attention and attract people to you. If possible, keep the centre of a room or building clear and open to allow this energy space to move.

WEST

7

Early evening
Autumn
Lake
Youngest daughter

The harvest activity of the autumn makes this chi energy ideal for bringing things to a profitable conclusion. It also helps you to be more content, relaxed and financially aware. The youngest daughter is associated with being playful and enjoying the pleasures of life, so this chi energy is good for romance and having an enjoyable, loving relationship.

NORTH

1

Night
Midwinter
Water
Middle son

This energy is helpful for being more independent, objective, spiritual and artistic. Ideal for conception, improving your sex life and any sleeping problems, your health and vitality are particularly influenced by this chi energy. It is a flexible energy that helps you deal with life's obstacles.

NORTH-WEST

6

Late evening
Autumn changing to winter
Heaven
Father

Having the most yang trigram and father as the family member, this energy represents experience and maturity, so is good for fostering leadership, responsibility and organization. It also encourages greater wisdom, clearer intuition and dignity, making it easier to win people's trust and respect.

problem

I'm often late for appointments because I find it difficult to wake up and get out of bed in the morning. How can I use Feng Shui to improve this situation?

solution

Sleep is a time for releasing the stress of the day's activities and for regenerating yourself. If you cannot wake up in the morning, it may be because you are deficient in the chi energy of the east, an energy associated with springtime, the sun rising and the beginning of the day.

If you think your problem stems from not being able to relax sufficiently at night, check that you do not have any mirrors facing you while you are asleep. This is because mirrors tend to reflect your own chi energy back at you rather than let you release it.

To ensure that your chi energy is not wasted on digestion, rather than getting you ready for the next day, make sure that you eat at least three hours before you go to bed. You should also use 100 per cent cotton bed linen as this will not generate a static charge of electricity that can upset your personal chi energy.

To expose yourself to more eastern energy, sleep with the top of your head pointing in this direction. If possible, sleep in the eastern part of your home in a room that has an east-facing window. Wooden surfaces and bright green tall objects all contain eastern energy, so a bedroom that has green walls or green bed linen, tall green leafy plants and a wooden floor or bed will also help you to feel refreshed and enthusiastic in the mornings.

EAST

Although it is usually advisable to close the curtains at night, I suggest you keep them open as this will expose you to vibrant morning sunshine chi energy, which will help you to get up. To feel more awake once you are out of bed, scrub your skin with a hot, damp cotton hand towel as this will stimulate your circulation. Open a few windows once you are up so that you will be revitalized by fresh air, and stretch and breathe deeply to invigorate your body. Eating your breakfast facing east or south-east will also help you to feel more awake and alert.

Getting out of bed will be easiest to achieve when your Nine Ki year number is in an eastern or south-eastern phase.

solution

The atmosphere of your bedroom has a significant influence on the quality of your sleep; the gentler and calmer the flow of chi energy there, the easier it will be to relax and fall into a deep sleep. To encourage this flow of chi energy, you need to make your bedroom more yin and increase the presence of water chi energy, which is related to night-time.

To create a cosy, yin atmosphere in your bedroom, decorate it with lots of soft fabrics and furnishings. A wool rug, flowing curtains and large cushions are good options. Cream is the most yin and peaceful of colours, so increase the presence of it in your bedroom to help overcome insomnia. You can complement cream with pastel shades of green and blue, both of which are also yin, relaxing colours.

Lots of large, leafy plants in your bedroom will calm the flow of energy at night and help you to fall asleep. To encourage a tranquil and intimate mood, keep the bedroom door and curtains closed at night. Mirrors speed up the flow of chi energy by bouncing it about a room, so if you have a mirror in your bedroom, remove it or cover it up at night. Synthetic fabrics carry a static charge of electricity that will adversely influence your chi energy and provoke an unsettled night's sleep, so make sure that all bed clothes and linen are made from pure cotton or other natural fabrics.

Chi energy is quietest in the north or north-west of your home, so if you have a choice of bedrooms, choose one that is in one of these directions. To align yourself with the peaceful water chi energy, position your bed so that the top of your head is pointing north.

To bring your chi energy down from your head – an action that calms your mind – soak your feet in very hot water for about ten minutes just before going to bed. Avoid stimulants such as coffee in the late afternoon and evening, or try replacing them with more calming beverages like camomile tea or hot apple juice.

I have been under a lot of stress at work and am having trouble getting to sleep, then staying asleep. I notice that when I stay at my girlfriend's house I don't have this problem. What can I do to my bedroom to help me sleep better at my home?

problem

I recently moved to a new home and have been experiencing a lot of nightmares. I wondered if the two are related and, if so, what Feng Shui can do to help me?

solution

Nightmares can often disrupt sleep and prevent your body from releasing the stresses and strains of the previous day. From a Feng Shui perspective, nightmares are mostly due to chi energy moving around the bedroom too quickly. This is made worse if the chi moves in a straight line and is directed towards the bed.

To calm the flow of chi energy in the bedroom, keep a rubber plant or any other plant with rounded floppy leaves in the room, especially in front of any protruding corners or sharp objects that point towards your bed. Bright colours, such as red, orange and purple, speed up the flow of chi energy, so try to decorate your bedroom with softer colours instead. Pale greens and blues are particularly good for fostering relaxing chi energy.

To align yourself with a more calming and peaceful energy, turn your bed so that the top of your head points in a north, north-west or west direction. If you have a choice of bedrooms, use a room to the north, north-west or west of the centre of your home.

To subdue the movement of chi energy in your bedroom at night, keep the door closed when you go to sleep. Removing or covering up any mirrors that face your bed will prevent chi energy from being reflected back at you while you sleep.

Another possible cause of nightmares is overexposure to electromagnetic fields (EMF). These fields radiate from any electrical equipment, for example, electric blankets, electric clocks, lights and televisions. To prevent exposure to EMF while you sleep, try to ensure that electrical equipment is switched off and is positioned as far away from your bed as possible.

things to avoid

If your bedroom is at the end of a long corridor or in the north-eastern part of your home, it will cause fast-moving and piercing chi energy to be directed at you while you sleep. This can make you feel as if you are under attack and will therefore encourage nightmares, so avoid this situation if possible.

WEALTH

2

problem

I feel I am dependent on others for basic financial advice and would like to be more financially aware. What can I do in terms of Feng Shui?

solution

The water chi energy of the north is associated with independence and objectivity, so exposure to this will stop you from relying heavily on other people's opinions. It also encourages money to flow towards you. To activate northern chi energy, fix a metal wind chime by a door in the north, or hang a crystal under a skylight in the north of your home. Wearing cream clothing and accessories will also surround you in more northern chi energy.

Western chi energy is also helpful as it relates to metal, the element of money, making you more aware of money and encouraging you to take more of an interest in financial matters. It may also help you to communicate better with your bank manager and keep track of financial accounts more thoroughly. To gain more exposure to western chi energy, sleep with the top of your head pointing west and, when possible, sit so you are facing this direction. You can also place a metal bowl filled with coins on a red cloth in the west of your home; a mirror behind the bowl will strengthen this energy even more.

To increase the presence of metal chi energy, add more red, gold and silver to your home by having curtains, fabrics, paintings and other objects in these colours. Red is also a more yang colour, so decorating your home with red objects and fabrics will help you to be more focused on your finances generally.

North-western chi energy encourages you to feel more organized and in control of your finances. Because the north-west is associated with heaven and the related trigram represents the father, increased exposure to this energy will enable you to approach financial matters with a sense of wisdom and dignity. As a result, you are less likely to rely on others for advice. To generate more north-western chi energy, place a pendulum clock or a round clock with as many metal parts as possible in the north-west of your home. To enhance it even further, put coins on a red cloth in a metal bowl in the north-west of your home and sleep so that the top of your head is pointing north-west.

It will be easiest for you to feel more aware and in control of your finances when your Nine Ki year number is in the west or north-west.

solution

Exposure to the quick, reactive chi energy of the north-east is ideal for helping you find new ways of generating wealth and acting on them before others. Being more yang will further encourage you to be more alert to financial opportunities.

There are a number of things you can introduce into your home to further enhance the energy of the north-east. For example, this direction is associated with mountains, so try placing decorative stones or rocks in and around your home. It is also associated with the colour brilliant white, so you can even go to the lengths of painting the walls and ceiling of your home this colour to bring out more of this energy. An easier way is to decorate your home with white flowers or white crystal rocks.

Fire chi energy nourishes north-eastern chi energy and is helpful for being able to determine future trends. To increase your exposure to fire chi energy, decorate your home with fabrics and objects that are made of bright, fiery purple colours, and include some bright lighting in the south. Keeping lots of plants with pointed leaves will also stimulate the presence of fire chi energy in your home.

To feel more alert to new opportunities, surround yourself in a more yang atmosphere. This can be achieved by having lots of open spaces, hard surfaces and bright colours in your home. At the same time, avoid having more yin features, such as low, comfy chairs, thick carpets and other heavy fabrics in your home.

Being high up gives you a feeling of space and encourages your own chi energy field to expand, with the result that you have a bigger view of opportunities. For this reason, you may find that working or living in a tall building is helpful, especially if the building that you occupy is taller than the ones surrounding it. On a more practical level, try to sit in tall chairs when you have the option. This could be a bar stool in your kitchen or a high stool at your work station.

The best times for taking advantage of opportunities are when your Nine Ki year number is in the north-east, west and south.

problem

I have missed some good investment opportunities recently. What kind of atmosphere would encourage me to be quicker and sharper at spotting new ways of making money?

problem

I run a business and we need to increase our profits. We have a good product with full orders, however, I know we could be more profitable. I would be interested in hearing some Feng Shui advice.

solution

The Feng Shui solution to this problem would be to enhance your exposure to the chi energies of the west and south-east. The energy of the west is associated with the harvest and will help you to reap greater financial rewards. The energy of the south-east relates to the sun rising and springtime, ensuring growth, progress and future prosperity.

One of the easiest ways to increase your exposure to western and south-eastern chi energy is by sleeping with the top of your head pointing in one of these directions, especially if you are the person who has the greatest influence over company profits. This may help you to introduce new procedures to improve the financial management of the company.

It will also be helpful if you face the west or south-east while you are working. If you employ other staff, consider arranging their workstations so that they also face one of these directions, especially accounting staff and others who deal directly with the flow of money. Ideally, it would be beneficial to conduct all accounting activities in the west of your office and to keep the safe containing cheques and cash waiting to be banked in this direction as well. Pinning a list of your financial goals in the west of your office may also help to improve profits by keeping your mind focused on achieving this objective.

To activate more western chi energy, keep red flowers in a round silver vase or coins on a red cloth in the west of your office. Placing a mirror behind the flower arrangement so that the back of it faces west will further stimulate this beneficial energy. The west is associated with metal, so make sure doorknobs and other metal handles in this area of your home are well polished in order to activate more metal chi energy.

To increase south-eastern chi energy, place an indoor fountain in this direction of your office. Green will enhance south-eastern chi energy, so decorate your office with green fabrics and objects.

The best time to undertake these changes will be when your Nine Ki year number is in the west or south-east.

One way of boosting the beneficial metal chi energy of the west is to keep coins tied with red cloth in this part of your home. You should also make sure that any metal objects in this area, such as door handles, are kept shiny.

solution

North-eastern chi energy encourages you to be more motivated and goal-oriented, while western chi energy helps you to be aware of your finances. The chi energy of the south-east is also useful because it allows you to get on with the kind of work that can make you wealthy. Another option is to make your environment and lifestyle slightly more yang as this will help you to become more active and motivated.

To absorb more of the chi energies of the north-east, west and south-east, turn your bed so that you sleep with the top of your head pointing in one of these directions. The chi energy of the north-east is the least compatible with deep sleep, so only try this direction if you find that the others are having little effect.

To activate western chi energy, keep red flowers in a round, silver container or coins in a metal bowl on a red cloth in the west part of your home. If you want to increase the energy of the north-east more, place white rocks or a white flowering plant in this part of your home. A water feature in the south-east of your home will nourish south-eastern chi energy. Growing lots of plants in all these areas of your home will keep the surrounding chi energy generally healthy. If the entrance to your home is in one of these directions, you will already have more of the chi energy of that particular direction.

To create a more yang environment, decorate your home with bright colours and keep surfaces clean and uncluttered. You can keep your personal chi energy more yang by eating plenty of root vegetables, grains and fish, or get involved in more yang activities such as martial arts for a while.

If you feel generally short of get-up-and-go, try to identify a few material items or achievements that would motivate you in life, then find pictures of these to keep in your home as a reminder. Photos of a holiday destination, an attractive car or country retreat are some examples. If possible, hang these pictures in the north-east, south-east or west of your home.

problem

I feel I would be more motivated in life if I set my sights more clearly on financial goals. How would you suggest I organize my office and home to achieve this?

Decorating with bright colours and eating more yang foods will help you to become more motivated. A water feature in the south-east of your home or office will also help.

problem

I am trying to sell my home for a good price. What Feng Shui solutions will help me do this?

solution

A determining factor in deciding to buy a home is the ambience people experience when viewing it. You therefore need to create an atmosphere that prospective buyers will feel happy living in.

The first thing to do is create a feeling of space. You can do this by storing away non-essential furniture and other free-standing items in a garage or at a friend's house. The more empty your home is, the bigger it will seem and this is always an attractive feature for potential buyers. It will also allow chi energy to flow more freely throughout the place. If you have narrow corridors or rooms in your home, place large mirrors in these areas to make them appear bigger. Don't have a mirror facing another mirror, door or window, however, as this will cause chi energy to become disoriented and chaotic.

The next thing to do is to give your home a thorough spring clean: this will refresh the chi energy and make your home feel more inviting. Rugs, carpets and curtains collect dust, mildew, smells and general stagnant chi energy, so wash these as well. If they look unattractive or old afterwards, they may put off potential buyers, in which case you should remove them completely.

To add colour and encourage a more healthy, natural atmosphere in your home, keep lots of plants and fresh flowers about the place. If your home is dark, you can brighten it with up-lights in the corners of rooms. Painting all the walls, ceilings and woodwork white will also help to make your home appear light, bright and clean. Cream is a more yin and relaxing colour, whereas a brilliant white creates a more stimulating, yang atmosphere, so choose the shade of white according to your individual requirements.

You may find it easier to sell your home when your Nine Ki year number is to the south-west, west or north-east.

solution

Immersing yourself in western metal chi energy, an energy that helps you to become more aware of your finances, will be the key to achieving this aim. In addition, you can also absorb more south-eastern tree energy, which is helpful for being positive and coming up with new ideas to make more money.

To absorb more of these energies, sleep with the top of your head pointing in one of these directions. The south-east is better if you are trying to build up wealth from scratch, whereas the west is preferable if you are consolidating the wealth you already have. Facing these directions when you are sitting at work or relaxing at home is another way to soak up their energies.

To enhance the energy of the south-east, place a water feature in this direction of your home. A moving water feature, such as an indoor water fountain, will be more yang and therefore help you to become more proactive about making money. As the south-east is associated with the tree element, placing lots of tall plants in this part of your home will further enhance this energy. Keep the area clean and tidy to allow chi energy to flow freely.

To increase the chi energy of the west, decorate this area of your home and office with objects that are red, metal or round. Shiny coins or silver plates displayed on a red cloth, and red flowers in a metal vase are good examples. In general, make sure that all metal items in your home and office, including door knockers and handles, are well polished as this will speed up the flow of western metal chi energy.

Items and objects that you bought during lean times, for example, second-hand furniture, may retain the very energy you are trying to get away from, so I suggest that you replace them with something new.

It will be easiest to create greater wealth when your Nine Ki year number is in the south-east or west.

problem

I want to create greater wealth in my life and wish to try Feng Shui. What should I do?

Keeping red, metal or shiny round objects in the west of your home is one way of enhancing western chi energy, which is beneficial for generating wealth.

nine ki astrology

Most of the remedies suggested in this book are based on rearranging various aspects of your home or work space to enhance the flow of propitious chi energy. Sometimes, however, the source of the problem may be due to bad timing, in which case you can use Nine Ki astrology to identify the best (and worst) times to achieve your aims.

There are two types of Feng Shui astrology and the one I use in this book is the Nine Ki system that is commonly used in Japan. The other system, often referred to as the Four Pillars, has a long history of use in China. I use Nine Ki astrology to help me make all major decisions and, in my experience, I have found that it helps me to achieve more with less effort. If you can have the forces of nature working for you rather than against you, everything becomes easier.

YOUR NINE KI YEAR NUMBER

Just as your birth date determines your star sign under the Western system of astrology, it also determines what is known as your year number under the Nine Ki system of astrology.

Your Nine Ki year number represents the pattern of chi energy present in the universe when you were born. This pattern of energy helped to shape your character and will stay with you for life. The energy patterns of each year change, however, and these mix with your personal chi energy each subsequent year to influence the way you feel and interact with people and places. Nine Ki astrology therefore allows you to predict the way you will feel in the future and you can use this to achieve your goals at a time when you are most likely to succeed.

Because energy patterns change each year on a nine-year cycle, there are nine different year numbers in Nine Ki astrology. To find out your year number, you need to make the following simple calculation. First, add together the last two digits of your year of birth. If the result is a two-digit number (that is, between 10 and 18) add the two digits again so that you end up with a number between 1 and 9.

If you were born between the years 1900 and 1999, subtract the result of this first calculation from 10. For birthdays in the year 2000 and beyond, subtract from 9. This final number is your Nine Ki year number. For example, if you were born in 1963, your Nine Ki year number is 1 (6+3=9, 10-9=1). If you were born in 1979, your Nine Ki year number is 3 (7+9=16, 1+6=7, 10-7=3). Someone born in the year 2000 will have a Nine Ki year number of 9 (0+0=0, 9-0=9).

According to the Nine Ki calendar, the beginning of the year is on the third, fourth or fifth of February, so if you were born in January or during the first two days of February, you

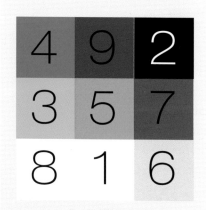

This matrix of numbers, known as the Magic Square, forms the basis of Nine Ki astrology. It serves as both a map and a timetable to chart the changing patterns of chi energy, which helps you to determine fortuitous occasions.

When your year number occupies a particular direction, you are more likely to achieve aims that require the attitude or emotion of that particular direction (see box below right).

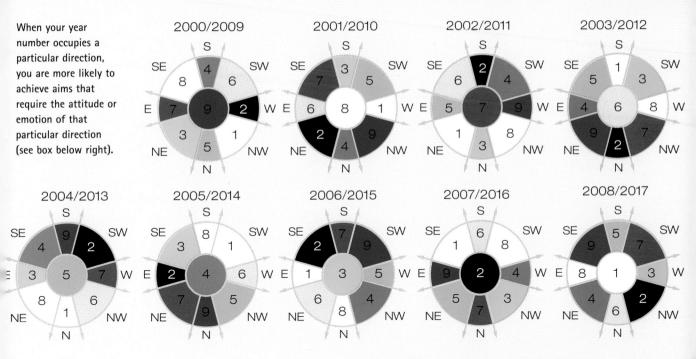

will need to base your calculations on the previous year. For example, if you were born on February 1, 1972, you need to calculate as if you were born in 1971, so the calculation would be 7+1=8, 10-8= Nine Ki year number 2.

TIMING EVENTS FOR PROPITIOUS RESULTS

Each year, your Nine Ki year number occupies a direction in one of the nine charts that represent the nine basic patterns of chi energy (see box above). Each direction is related to a certain type of emotion or attitude (see box right) and if your Nine Ki year number occupies that direction or phase, then you are more likely to achieve aims that require the attitude or emotion of that particular direction.

For example, if your Nine Ki year number is 7, look at which direction it occupies in the year charts above. In the year 2001, 7 is in the south-east, which means you will be influenced by south-eastern chi energy. The south-east is associated with being creative, imaginative, persistent and communicative, so it should be easier to find a new job or attract a suitable partner in the year 2001.

DIRECTION	EMOTION
North	Independent, peaceful, spiritual, flexible, affectionate, objective
South-west	Practical, realistic, intimate, close, caring
East	Enthusiastic, ambitious, active, confident, focused
South-east	Creative, imaginative, persistent, communicative
Centre	Powerful, changeable, forceful, attention-seeking
North-west	Dignified, self-disciplined, self-assured, organized, in control
West	Content, pleasure-seeking, romantic, fun-loving, financially aware
North-east	Motivated, quick, decisive, competitive, open to change
South	Expressive, emotional, generous, sociable, noticeable

problem

Although I earn a good salary, I never seem to have anything to show for it. I am concerned that in the long term I will have acquired no lasting wealth. What are the Feng Shui remedies to this problem?

solution

The chi energy of the south-west relates to autumn time and is similar to the kind of energy that encourages squirrels and other animals to store food for the winter. By immersing yourself in this type of energy, you will be better able to conserve and consolidate your earnings.

To absorb more south-western chi energy, sleep with the top of your head pointing in this direction for a while. Facing this direction when you are relaxing at home or working in your office will also help. To enhance south-western chi energy, decorate this part of your home with yellow or matt black objects and fabrics. Freshly cut yellow flowers are one of the easiest ways to introduce the colour yellow into this area. The south-west is associated with soil, so having a clay pot filled with charcoal in this direction will also add more of this energy to your home.

To prevent overspending and encourage you to save money, ensure there are no leaks, mildew or dampness in bathrooms, kitchens and toilets, especially if they are in the west or south-west of your home. Keep these rooms clean, dry and as empty as possible. Metal is the element related to money, so add more of this chi energy in the west of your home by decorating with silver, grey or off-white colours.

If your stairs lead down to your front door or you can see the back door from the front door, chi energy will drain from your house more easily, preventing you from building up lasting wealth. To discourage this, keep bushy plants close by or place a small convex mirror (5cm or less in diameter) where you can see it as you descend your stairs or walk towards your back door.

When your Nine Ki year number is in the south-west, you will find it much easier to acquire lasting wealth.

Charcoal in a clay pot and yellow and matt black objects kept in the south-west of your home will help you to conserve and consolidate your earnings.

just
common sense

When you spend money, buy things that will hold or increase their value over the years. Antiques, paintings, classic cars, property and jewellery all have the potential to do this.

solution

To save money, you will need to make sure that the atmosphere in your home is conducive to being financially aware and to using money effectively. In Feng Shui, the chi energies of the south-west and west will foster this atmosphere.

To activate more south-western chi energy, place yellow flowers or a yellow flowering plant in this part of your home. The flowers will be more effective if they are kept in a clay container because clay has soil chi energy, a Five Element that is related to the south-west. To activate more western chi energy, keep coins, your cheque book, red flowers or a red flowering plant in the west of your home.

To expose yourself to an energy that will help with self-discipline and planning ahead, position your chair so that you are sitting in the north-west of your room facing south-east. You can also align yourself with this energy by sleeping with the top of your head pointing north-west.

You can lose wealth by letting energy flow out of your home too easily. The chances of this happening will increase if you have leaky taps or leave water running, so if the plumbing in your home is faulty, fix it as soon as possible. To minimize the loss of chi energy in the bathroom, keep the lid on your lavatory down when you flush and keep the bathroom door closed at all times. Dampness or mildew can cause stagnant, negative chi, so keep plants in your bathroom to absorb excess moisture.

problem

Are there any Feng Shui tips for saving money? I earn a good salary, but it always seems to slip through my fingers far too easily.

I tend to be too careless and reckless with money. I'm an impulsive shopper and often regret my purchases. What Feng Shui solutions would improve my situation?

solution

The quick-changing chi energy of the north-east can encourage you to be more impulsive, while the thundery, active chi energy of the east can cause you to be careless. To curb your impulse-buying you need to calm these energies and immerse yourself in more north-western energy, which has a more structured, organized quality that will help you to take a long-term view of your spending. Absorbing more south-western chi energy will encourage you to be more practical and careful with your purchases, which can also help to solve your problem.

To calm north-eastern chi energy, place ramekin dishes filled with two tablespoons of sea salt in the north-east part of your home. Decorating this area with objects, fabrics or flowers that are pink or grey will further help to subdue this energy. Eastern chi energy can be quietened by using candles instead of lights in this part of your home and by decorating with very pale greens or blues. If there is a front or back door in the east or north-east of your home, these energies will be more abundant and fast-flowing, in which case you should place a bushy plant by the door, which will have a calming effect.

To increase your exposure to north-western chi energy, place a round, metal pendulum clock in this direction of your home. Keeping silver objects, a coin collection or items that are coloured grey here will also strengthen this energy.

To enhance south-western chi energy, place yellow flowers and spreading plants, such as violets and begonias, in this part of your home. Soil is the Five Element related to the south-west, so placing charcoal in a clay container in this direction will further strengthen this beneficial chi energy.

A yang atmosphere will make it harder to overcome problems, so create a more yin atmosphere by incorporating floppy-leaved plants, pale colours and soft fabrics in your home. At the same time, avoid having hard surfaces, mirrors, crystals and sharp corners.

It will be easier to control your spending when your Nine Ki year number is in the north-west or south-west.

Decorating the north-east of your home with pink and grey colours will calm the detrimental chi energy of this direction, making you less inclined to act on impulse.

solution

Retirement signals the end of one cycle and the beginning of another. In Feng Shui, the chi energies of the west and north-west are most useful in helping you to complete cycles satisfactorily. Western chi energy is more playful and therefore better if you want to be relaxed and feel good about life while you make the transition. North-western chi energy is preferable if you want to bring your wisdom to new projects, for instance, if you want to become a consultant or get involved in a local charity.

To absorb more western chi energy, face this direction when you are sitting down and turn your bed so that the top of your head is pointing in this direction when you sleep. To activate more western chi energy in your home, keep red flowers in a round silver vase, shiny coins placed on a red cloth, or red ribbons in this area. You can also position a mirror so that its back is facing the west.

To increase north-western chi energy, put a pendulum clock with as many metal parts as possible, round silver dishes or a round metal-framed mirror in this part of your home. You can also turn your bed so that your head is pointing in this direction when you sleep.

A year when your Nine Ki year number is in the west or north-west is the ideal time to take retirement.

I am planning to retire in the next few years and want to make the transition from having a regular income to not having one as smooth as possible. What can I do to achieve this?

just common sense

When the time comes and you want to make the transition from working to retirement as quickly as possible, store or throw away all items that relate to your work and seek out new activities. Taking up painting, gardening, further study or a sport will give you a focus in life and prevent you from feeling that you are missing out.

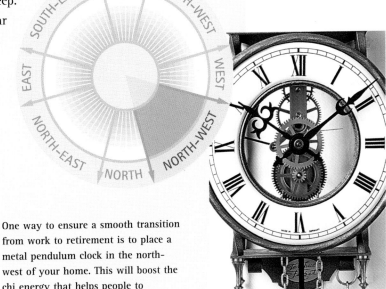

One way to ensure a smooth transition from work to retirement is to place a metal pendulum clock in the north-west of your home. This will boost the chi energy that helps people to complete life cycles successfully.

plants

Healthy growing plants are unique Feng Shui features because they bring natural, live chi energy into your home. This is particularly important as modern rooms are becoming increasingly filled with synthetic and sometimes toxic materials like MDF (medium density fibre), plastics and paints. Plants also release oxygen, so they are one of the most effective ways of introducing clean, fresh air into a room.

Generally, plants are classified as adding tree chi energy to a space. However, depending on the type, some plants have more of one kind of energy than others. By buying the appropriate plants and placing them in a room, you can increase your exposure to the kinds of chi energy you think will benefit you most. In my opinion, as long as you have the space, the more plants the better.

Plants are a simple way to solve problem areas in your home. For example, if there is a line of doors along a corridor or doors or windows opposite each other, chi energy speeds up, which makes a space less relaxing. By staggering plants along the corridor or placing bushy plants close to the windows or doors, the chi will slow down.

Plants with pointy leaves, such as the butterfly palm (below left), radiate more yang energy. Plants with narrow, droopy leaves, such as a spider plant, (below right) generate yin energy. Bushy, leafy plants, such as the ficus (left), slow down fast-moving chi. Trailing plants, such as an ivy plant (below middle) create more water chi energy.

Stairs leading to a front door also cause chi to flow too quickly. Fast-flowing chi can create a deficiency of chi in the whole building, which may make it harder for you to develop your wealth. This problem can be remedied by placing a bushy plant between

the foot of your stairs and the front door. Another example is the oppressive, downward-flowing chi that is found in a room with heavy beams. This can encourage depression and a pessimistic outlook, but placing tall, pointy-leaved plants in the room will remedy the situation.

Finally, it is most common for chi energy to stagnate in the corners of a room. To help speed up the movement of chi energy in corners, you can place plants that have strong, pointed leaves there. The fiery energy these kinds of plants have will also make the room more lively.

flowers

Fresh flowers not only radiate living chi energy, they also brings to a room the chi energy associated with their particular colour (see pages 114–15) and, to a lesser extent, their shape. Just by introducing flowers into a room, you can bring about a significant change to the existing chi energy there. And because there are so many different varieties, you can alter the energy of a room simply by choosing different-coloured flowers.

Always throw flowers away before they start wilting because dying flowers radiate a negative, decaying chi energy into your home or workspace. In my opinion, it is fine to use dried flowers once they have thoroughly dried out and stabilized, but they will not be as effective as living flowers. Similarly, artificial flowers will not carry living chi energy, so do not substitute them for real ones.

Yellow flowers are good decorations to have when entertaining guests because they create a lively, sociable chi energy that is conducive to deepening friendships.

North	North-east	East	South-east	South	South-west	West	North-west
Orchids mixed with red flowers can revive a dull sex life	Lily of the valley flowers are calming	Ferns enhance vitality and freshness	Cornflowers help you to communicate better and encourage travel	Clematis encourage passion and success	Pansies foster contentment and family harmony	Roses boost romance and tulips help to generate wealth	Pompon dahlias enhance dignity and wisdom

problem

It isn't easy for me to spend money on myself. I always think I don't need something. What can I do to make myself feel more comfortable about treating myself well?

things to avoid

Exposure to a lot of north-western chi energy can make you too serious and responsible about money. To avoid this energy, don't sleep with the top of your head pointing in this direction. You can also calm this energy in your home by keeping cream-coloured objects and glass or translucent surfaces in this part of your home.

solution

Depending on the underlying cause of this problem, you can increase your exposure to a variety of different energies. Western chi energy will help you to be more hedonistic; north-eastern chi energy will encourage you to put your own needs before others; the springtime, sunrise energy of the east will increase your confidence and assertiveness; and the water chi energy of the north that is associated with flexibility will help you to develop a more 'happy-go-lucky' attitude to money.

Once you have decided which of these energies to concentrate on, turn your bed so that you sleep with the top of your head pointing in the direction of that energy. Similarly, when you sit down at work, face one of these directions to absorb more of that energy.

To increase the presence of western energy in your home, keep freshly cut red flowers in a metal vase there. To enhance north-eastern energy, place white rock crystals in this part of your home or workspace. To boost eastern chi energy, place a bowl of fresh water or another type of water feature in the east of your home. Finally, to foster more northern chi energy, place a mirror there.

Living in a yin environment will help you to feel more relaxed about spending money on yourself. To create a yin atmosphere at home, soften any sharp corners or edges of furniture by placing bushy plants in front of them. Lots of plants with floppy leaves around your home in general will slow the flow chi energy. Comfortable furnishings are also yin, so decorate your home with big cushions and upholstered armchairs. You can also eat more vegetables, salads and fruit and pursue relaxing activities such as t'ai chi or yoga.

It will be hardest to indulge yourself when your Nine Ki number is in the north-west, so wait until the next year when your Nine Ki year number will be in the west.

Eating light meals and keeping comfortable furniture in your home will make you more yin, an energy that will encourage you to relax about treating yourself well.

solution

An inability to share is a sign that your personal chi energy is too confined. To enable your chi energy to be more expansive, avoid small rooms and other confined spaces. An overfurnished home or one that is decorated extensively with fabrics like heavy curtains, tablecloths and cushion covers will make you less outgoing and increase the risk of you wanting to hold onto things, so avoid these where possible. Similarly, avoid exposure to the colours brown, beige and dark yellow as these are associated with conserving what you have and will make it harder for you to share.

Being carefree and generous is associated with southern chi energy. To expose yourself to more of this chi energy, place purple-coloured objects in this area of your home and let plenty of sunlight in. Photographs or paintings of sunny scenes can inspire the kind of thought process that will generate more fire chi energy inside your body. In the evenings, you can light candles to create the same effect.

To become more flexible about your wealth, expose yourself to more water chi energy. The easiest way to achieve this is by placing a water feature in the east or south-east of your home. Ideally the water should be moving, so a small waterfall would be suitable. Cream colours, glossy surfaces and curvy objects in the form of furniture, glass sculptures or soft fabrics, placed around your home will also increase the presence of water chi energy.

Too much soil or metal chi energy associated with the south-west, west, north-west and north-east parts of your home can aggravate your problem, so make sure you keep these areas clean, tidy and free of clutter. Keeping the rest of your home tidy is also general good Feng Shui practice.

Try sleeping with the top of your head pointing south or north temporarily and see if you feel more carefree with your money as a result. You could also try sitting so that you face one of these directions when you relax. However, be careful not to adopt these directions in the long term because they can cause problems relating to excessive emotion and loneliness respectively.

I find it very hard to share my wealth. I know my friends think I am mean but I cannot find a way of being more carefree. How can Feng Shui help?

The fiery, passionate chi energy of the south will help you to become more carefree. To increase this chi energy, place purple objects in this direction of your home.

problem

I am so obsessed with finding ways of making more money that I rarely enjoy the money I have. Can you suggest anything to put in my office or home to help?

solution

This kind of obsession is related to the competitive, hard-working mountain chi energy of the north-east. To feel more relaxed about making money and to enjoy the lifestyle that you have already, you need to decrease your exposure to this type of energy and build up the chi energies of the south-west and west.

To reduce the amount of north-eastern chi energy in your home and office, place more yin and metal elements in the north-east – these will have a calming effect on the Five Element soil that is related to the north-east. You can also decorate this area with pink and light grey colours and place round-shaped objects, such as silver plates or coins there. Putting a ramekin dish filled with sea salt in the north-east of your home will also help to calm this energy. Do not sleep with the top of your head pointing towards the north-east and, similarly, avoid facing this direction when you are working.

If there is a front door or a main entrance in the north-east direction of your home or office, there will be a strong flow of north-eastern chi energy coming into the area. I would therefore advise you to place a metal wind chime over the door or lots of bushy plants by the doorstep to slow the flow of this detrimental energy.

The chi energy of the south-west is helpful for making the most of what you already have, while the energy of the west encourages you to feel content and enjoy the pleasures of life. To absorb more of either of these energies, sleep with the top of your head pointing in the appropriate direction or make sure you face it while you work.

Obsessive behaviour is a common symptom of being too yang. If chi energy is moving around you too fast, this will create a more yang atmosphere, so you need to slow the flow of chi energy. To do this, decorate your home with yin colours such as cream, pink, pale green or pale blue. You can also slow the flow of chi energy around sharp corners and in corridors by placing bushy plants there.

If corners from other buildings are pointing at your home, this will cause negative 'cutting' chi to flow in your direction. To avoid this, grow vegetation between the two buildings or place a small convex mirror or shiny metal plaque on the outside of your home, making sure that it points towards the offending corner.

solution

One Feng Shui solution to this problem would be to absorb more of the energy of the east. This will increase your confidence, which will discourage you from feeling uncomfortable about the money you earn. Exposing yourself to more of the fiery, bright, southern chi energy will encourage you to develop more pride in your earnings, and being surrounded in more northern chi energy will give you a more objective attitude to wealth.

To enhance all of these energies, place a bowl of fresh water in the east, keep lit candles in the south and hang a metal wind chime that can chime regularly or red ribbons in the north. If you want to absorb more of one particular energy, then you can turn your bed so that the top of your head is facing that direction when you sleep.

Becoming more yang will help you to change your attitude to money, so try to create a more yang atmosphere at home. Keep floors, tables and other surfaces well polished and clutter-free. Reducing the amount of furniture and fabrics that you have in your home will also help. To increase personal yang energy, dress in smarter clothes, wear jewellery and accessorize with bright colours.

It will be easiest to feel guilt-free about your money when your Nine Ki year number is in the east, south, west, north and north-east.

just
common sense

By viewing money as a way in which others value what you have to offer, you won't feel so guilty about earning so much. You can also spend it in such a way that improves the quality of everyone's lives, for example buying organic vegetables to reduce pollution.

problem

I earn a reasonable amount of money but I feel guilty about it. I often try to play down my wealth and hide it from others. I feel uneasy in the company of others who I suspect would be jealous. I would appreciate some help.

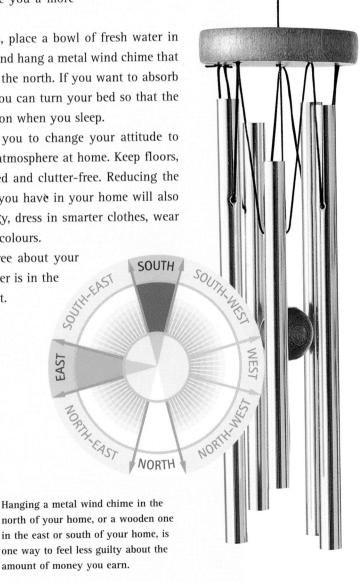

Hanging a metal wind chime in the north of your home, or a wooden one in the east or south of your home, is one way to feel less guilty about the amount of money you earn.

problem

I constantly fret about money and the future, although my friends and family say I have no reason. How could I be more relaxed about my ability to earn money?

solution

Worry and insecurity about financial matters can be a sign that you do not have enough confidence in yourself or your future generally. To enhance your self-esteem, try to create a more dynamic, yang environment. To do this, keep the rooms in your home clear of clutter, and decorate with bright colours. Vibrant, tall, pointy-leaved plants and mirrors placed in the east or south-east of your home will also help to generate more yang chi energy in your home.

The metal chi energy of the west is associated with greater awareness of how to make money. To activate this, keep red flowers, coins on a red cloth in a metal pot or a mirror in this area of your home. Decorating this direction of your home with red colours will also foster this beneficial energy.

The chi energy of the north can promote the feeling that money flows to you more easily. A crystal hung in a northern window, a metal wind chime over a northern door or growing ivy in the north of your home will therefore strengthen this chi energy and help you to achieve your aims.

The chi energy of the east is associated with self-confidence, and can help you to overcome any insecurities about earning money. To absorb more of this energy, place a water feature in the eastern part of your home or workplace, along with tall indoor plants. You can also use bright green colours to decorate this area.

Another way to reassure yourself of your ability to make money is by keeping reminders of your success on display in your home or office. Each time you see these items, you will be reminded of how you have triumphed in the past and will feel reassured of future financial success.

Placing a water feature in the east of your home and a mirror in the east or south-east will help you to develop more confidence about earning money. Decorating your home with bright colours will further help.

RELATIONSHIPS

problem

I am not a very outgoing person and spend a lot of time on my own. I frequently feel lonely as a result. Which Feng Shui solutions could help to change this situation?

solution

This problem is a sign that your chi energy is too quiet on the surface and you therefore lack the drive to meet new people. To feel more sociable, you need to expose yourself to more fiery yang energy. This energy is also associated with the south direction of the midday sun, so start by applying Feng Shui solutions in the southern part of your home.

Natural sunlight encourages fiery, sociable energy so if the south of your home doesn't have lots of windows, make sure you use bright up-lights there. Alternatively, you can light candles for a while each day there. To increase sociable energy in the south, south-west and north-east of your home, use purple-coloured flowers, fabrics or other objects. South-west chi energy is helpful for making long-term friendships and the north-east for being more outgoing generally.

To make the overall atmosphere of your house more yang, look for opportunities in your home where you can introduce brighter, yang colours such as red, yellow and purple. Plants with pointed leaves, such as yuccas, will also help to create a fiery atmosphere.

Overexposure to northern chi energy can also increase the risk of feeling isolated and lonely because it is an energy that is associated with the night and winter, and therefore stillness and quietness. Your home will receive more northern chi energy if its main entrance is to the north of your home or if your home faces north. If this is the case, you can paint your front door red to add a stronger yang colour.

There are also some directions in which you can sleep to help you absorb the kind of chi energy that makes it easier to meet people and make friends. Sleeping with the top of your head pointing south-east is helpful for being more communicative, imaginative and harmonious with people. Sleeping with the top of your head pointing south will help you to be expressive, outgoing and social. Sleeping with your head facing south-west will encourage intimacy and the ability to maintain deeper friendships.

It will be easier to be more social when your Nine Ki year number is in the south. Other good opportunities would be while your Nine Ki year number is to the north-east, south-east and south-west.

solution

To restore your friendship and encourage feelings of closeness, you and your friend should immerse yourselves in the settled chi energy of the south-west. Being in a yin environment will also help because yin energy reduces the risk of new confrontations and will encourage you to feel relaxed and at peace.

As you will be having a meal, focus your efforts on your dining room. To increase the presence of south-western chi energy in this room, add more of the colour yellow. Flowers are a good way to do this. Putting lots of fabrics in this room, such as tablecloths or rugs, will also help, as will growing lots of spreading plants, for example, begonia.

Try sitting on low chairs or cushions on the floor before you begin your meal at the dinner table. These items of furniture are more yin and will help you to relax and feel less confrontational. When you sit down at the dining table to eat, make sure you sit facing south-west. Other favourable directions to sit are facing west or south-east. Seating your friend opposite you can be rather confrontational, so I would suggest that you sit at an angle to each other. Neither of you should be facing south or north-east because this increases the risk of having arguments.

Protruding corners that point in your direction will cause fast flowing and unsettling chi energy to come your way, so soften corners with plants or fabrics. Similarly, make sure that neither of you is sitting close to a door or between a door and window, a situation that can encourage feelings of insecurity. It would be better to sit facing into the room, ideally with doors and windows in view.

To create a more yin atmosphere in the dining room, soften sharp corners, hard surfaces and mirrors by putting bushy plants in front of them. You can also use these kinds of plants to break up straight lines that cause chi energy to pick up speed and become more yang. Decorate the room with pastel-coloured objects to further encourage a more yin ambience. Candles create a softer yin atmosphere, so use these or low table lamps instead of overhead electric lighting.

In a year when your or your friend's Nine Ki year number is in the south, you may find a reconciliation harder to achieve. If this is the case, wait until the following year when it will be in the north.

problem

I want to invite a friend over for a meal with the aim of resolving a major dispute we had. What kind of atmosphere would be ideal for this?

problem

I notice that my dinner guests sometimes leave earlier than I would like. How can Feng Shui prevent this?

solution

The atmosphere of your dining room will have a significant effect on how comfortable your guests feel and, therefore, how long they will stay. If your dining room is decorated with bright colours, has shiny surfaces and a regimented layout, then it is too yang and your guests are likely to feel uncomfortable and leave early. Fast food restaurants are decorated in this way, which is ideal for attracting customers, then getting them to leave as soon as they have eaten.

Like all matters of yin and yang, however, there needs to be a balance. If you go too far the other way and decorate your dining room with lots of pastel colours and soft furnishings, the atmosphere will be too yin and relaxed. As a result, your guests may feel sleepy and nod off as the evening progresses.

To encourage dinner guests to stay longer, try to seat them around an oval or round table because this will encourage lively and interesting discussion. Make sure that none of your guests sits with his or her back to a sharp, protruding corner - the cutting chi this situation causes will make it harder for him or her to relax. Candles give off a softer light, which makes the atmosphere more warm and intimate. You can also use indirect lighting, such as up-lights reflected off your ceiling, to create this feeling. Shiny cutlery, cut glass and red napkins will add sparkle and excitement to the evening.

Exposure to a variety of atmospheres will increase the chances of your guests staying for longer so, where possible, use more than one room when entertaining. For example, serve drinks and snacks in your living room, then move to the dining room for the meal, then back to the living room for coffee. In this situation it would be helpful to make your living room as yin and comfortable as possible with soft, comfortable chairs, big cushions and a real fire. Closing the doors will add to the cosiness. A yin living room will balance the more dynamic, yang atmosphere of your dining room.

solution

If you want to host a fun party, the best time to hold it would be a couple of days before a full moon. This is a very yang time when people become more outgoing, dynamic and in the mood for a party. Also, more guests are likely to turn up if the party is around the full moon.

To create a lively party atmosphere, you need to make space in your home so that chi energy can move freely. To do this, empty the rooms you intend to use as much as possible by moving any non-essential furniture out of the way. Your guests are more likely to get up and dance if there is space and the chi energy is moving about quickly.

If there are rugs on the floor, take them up because bare floors allow chi energy to flow more quickly. Lots of shiny, reflective objects will also encourage fast-flowing chi energy, so hang a mobile made from shiny metal shapes, a mirrored ball or a crystal from the ceiling: these will make the chi energy spin in lots of different directions. Large mirrors are also good for creating fast-flowing energy and give the illusion that there is greater space and more people at the party.

To give the main party room a more stimulating ambience, decorate it with reds, purples and other bright, yang colours. You can introduce these colours into the room with fresh-cut flowers, party decorations or coloured lighting.

If your home is big enough, set up another room for people who prefer to mingle and chat, rather than dance. This second room should have a more yin atmosphere, so make sure it contains soft furnishings, rugs and plants. Comfortable chairs, big floor cushions and lit candles will encourage people to make conversation with each other. Make sure the temperature in this room is warm as this will foster intimacy.

problem

I want to hold a party in my home for a good friend. Do you have any suggestions to help make it a memorable occasion?

The colour purple encourages lively, yang energy, so decorate your home with purple objects if you want guests to dance. If you prefer a more intimate ambience, have lit candles and soft furnishings. This creates a yin atmosphere, which encourages guests to relax and mingle.

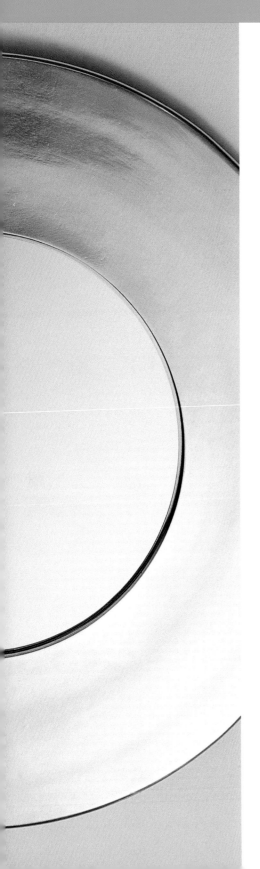

mirrors

Mirrors speed up the flow of chi energy, creating a more dynamic, stimulating and yang atmosphere, and encouraging you to feel more excited. It is therefore a useful tool to manipulate chi energy in order to helps solve problems. Too many mirrors in your home, however, can make it harder for you to feel relaxed or settled there.

Mirrors and other reflective surfaces change the direction of chi energy in the same way that light is reflected in different directions. This makes them especially effective when you want to disperse fast-moving chi energy or reflect chi energy into a stagnant area, and I often recommend mirrors as a Feng Shui solution to problems. Flat mirrors are better for reflecting energy evenly around a room, whereas convex mirrors (see page 136) disperse chi energy in many different directions. Objects made from a polished reflective metal, such as door knockers, knobs and handles; polished metal pots and pans; and light fittings can also disperse energy in different directions.

Because mirrors reflect light back into an area, they are particularly useful features to have in spaces that don't have a lot of light, such as basements or north-facing rooms. They also help to make narrow rooms feel larger, especially if the mirrors are floor-to-ceiling. To make a room appear twice as wide, place large mirrors along one of the longer walls. The same effect can be achieved in corridors by staggering the placement of mirrors on each side. For a more even flow of chi energy along a corridor, place a plant or tapestry opposite each mirror as this will slow the flow of chi energy.

Another use for mirrors is to make up for any of the energies of the Eight Directions that appear deficient in your home or workplace. Look at your floor plan and see if any of the Eight Directions fall in a corner (especially in the case of an L-shaped home), indentation or any other complicated shape. Place a mirror in the area where there is deficient chi energy, making sure that the back of the mirror faces the outside of your home, and not another room.

The shape and material of the frame should also be considered: a circular mirror with a metal frame will generate more yang, metal chi energy. The colour can also have a subtle effect (see pages 114–15).

HAZARDOUS MIRROR POSITIONS

Whenever you use mirrors it is important to avoid hanging them so that they directly face a door or window because this causes chi energy entering the building to be reflected back out again. Bear in mind, too, that you should not place two mirrors opposite each other because the chi will bounce back and forth, creating a tense atmosphere.

In general, avoid having mirrors in your bedroom because the more yang atmosphere they create is not conducive to good sleep. If you must have a mirror in your bedroom, position it so that it does not face your bed. This way, the emotions and chi energy you release during sleep won't be reflected back at you, and you will wake up feeling refreshed and rejuvenated.

Placing a mirror by an entrance will encourage chi energy to flow into and circulate around your home more easily.

crystals

Similar to mirrors, clear crystals help to spread chi energy in the same way that they refract light. A spherical, multi-faceted crystal hung in your window will catch the sunlight and spread a pattern of all the colours of the rainbow onto the walls around the room. Each reflected colour carries the chi energy relating to it, for example, green carries the chi energy of the east. Crystals are particularly useful Feng Shui tools when you need to increase chi energy in a room or part of a room.

As they are associated with water chi energy, crystals are also particularly helpful for becoming more objective and flexible. They are most effective if you hang them in the north, east or south-east of your home.

Crystals that have a piece of string or cotton thread attached to them will be easier to hang from ceilings and windows. You can also buy rock crystals that can be placed on window sills or corner tables.

problem

I have been single for some time. Although I meet lots of people, I have not been able to find the right person. What Feng Shui remedies can I try?

solution

The west is the direction associated with romance, so you should aim to enhance your exposure to the chi energy of this direction. You can do this by placing red objects, such as red ribbons or two red roses, in this area of your home. It would also help to activate the chi energies of the south-east and south-west as these encourage feelings of positivity and intimacy respectively. This can be achieved by keeping a bowl of fresh water in the south-east of your home (make sure you refill it with clean water each morning) and a yellow flowering plant in the south-west of your home. You can also absorb more of a particular energy if you sleep so that your head is pointing in that direction.

To stay focused in your search for the right person, it would be helpful to identify the qualities that you are looking for in a partner. Write these down on a piece of paper and keep this list somewhere prominent, preferably in the west of your home. You can also make a list of your own personality traits that you think others may find attractive in you and place it in the west of your home.

Another thing that may help you to attract a suitable partner is to change your home surroundings in such a way that it enhances your positive attributes and tones down your more negative ones. Turn to page 53 to find out which directions are associated with which characteristics and, therefore, to which energies you should increase or decrease your exposure. For example, if you think that others find you distant and not playful enough, you can decrease your exposure to northern chi energy by placing lots of plants in the north of your home, and increase your exposure to more western chi energy by having more shiny, metal objects in the west.

To develop the kind of personal chi energy that is conducive to being in a relationship, it would be helpful to keep pairs of decorative objects, such as candles, sculptures or two flowers in a vase, around your home. Displaying romantic pictures of couples will also help.

It will be easiest to find the right person when your Nine Ki year number is in the west or south-east.

To increase your exposure to romantic chi energy, place red objects, such as red roses, in the west of your home. You can also make a list of all the desirable qualities you are looking for in a partner and keep this in the west of your home, too.

solution

It is very rare to meet a person that fulfils all your expectations. In fact, one of the challenges of any relationship is working together to make it mutually satisfying. By accepting a relationship that is less than perfect, you will learn to adapt and compromise and, in the process, develop greater self-awareness. This will then help you to become a better, more well-rounded person.

You would probably feel more positive about your present partner if you increased your exposure to south-eastern chi energy. This direction relates to the morning and springtime, which are times when you are more likely to take a fresh look at things. You can generate more south-eastern energy by placing a bowl of fresh water in this part of your home. You can also absorb more of this energy if you turn your bed so that the top of your head is pointing south-east when you sleep.

I have very high expectations from a relationship. Perhaps I am too romantic, but I dream of the perfect lover and no one seems to match up. Is it possible to be more content with the relationship I am in?

The energy of the west is good for contentment, so make sure that this part of your home is clean, tidy and has lots of healthy plants to encourage the circulation of good chi energy there. Keeping a pair of red flowers in a silver-coloured vase in this direction will also boost your exposure to western chi energy.

South-western chi energy helps you to focus on improving the quality of what you already have, so try to absorb more of this energy as well. Keep a yellow flowering plant in a clay container or a pair of candles that you light regularly in the south-west of your home. Pairs of decorative objects will help to reinforce the feeling of being together. Bright lights and bright purple or yellow fabrics and decorative objects in this part of your home will also increase your exposure to south-western chi energy.

You are more likely to feel fulfilled in your relationship when your Nine Ki year number is in the south-west, west or south-east.

problem

I have been in a relationship for a year and, although we have a lot of fun, it seems a bit superficial. How can Feng Shui help me decide whether this is the right person for me?

Placing a statue of a laughing Buddha in the north or north-west of your home will enhance the chi energies of these directions and help you to make important decisions.

solution

Whenever you want to make an important decision, you should always try to absorb more north-western chi energy. This is because the north-west is associated with heaven, intuition and wisdom. At the same time, try to become slightly more yang as this energy will help you be more decisive and focus on the issues at hand.

To surround yourself in more north-western chi energy, keep a pendulum clock with as many metal parts as possible in this area of your home. Metal is the element related to the north-west, so any additional metal, round or silver-coloured objects here will further increase this energy. You can also absorb more north-western chi energy by sleeping with the top of your head pointing north-west or sitting so that you face this direction.

To immerse yourself in a more yang environment, create more open floor space and surfaces by clearing your home of all non-essential items. Having a good clear out of all cupboards, drawers and storage spaces will also disperse old chi energy and allow fresh new chi energy into your home, which will make it easier to see your relationship in a new light.

The chi energy of the north helps to foster feelings of objectivity and detachment, which are helpful when making important decisions such as the one you are facing. To boost northern energy in your life, hang a metal wind chime near a door in the north of your home or a crystal near a window in the north. This direction is associated with water chi energy, so placing glass or curvy-shaped items in this part of your home will also increase your exposure to northern chi energy.

Another way to increase the energies of the north and north-west is by placing a symbol of wisdom, such as a laughing Buddha, in one of these areas of your home. The Buddha needs to be placed at about head height within the room for it to be most effective.

It will be easiest to decide if you are in the right relationship when your Nine Ki number is to the north-west.

solution

If your partner seems indecisive about your future together and you are putting the pressure on for an answer, your lover may resist and the relationship may founder as a result. A better approach would be to just relax and focus on the fact that you have mutual love and respect for one another.

To be more relaxed about the whole issue, absorb more western chi energy. The west relates to the time of day when the sun starts to set and helps to foster feelings of contentment. To increase your own exposure to western chi energy, wear lots of red or pink clothes, metal jewellery or other personal accessories that are red or made with metal. If you have a room at home for your sole use, such as a study, keep pink flowers in the west of it and sit facing in a western direction.

If your partner is struggling to resolve the issue of commitment and is willing to use Feng Shui, increase his or her exposure to north-western chi energy. This energy is associated with fatherly wisdom and dignity, and is particularly helpful for planning ahead. To enhance north-western energy, place metal objects, such as a pendulum clock, or grey, silver and off-white objects in the north-west of your home. Your partner can also absorb more of this energy by wearing accessories that are grey, silver and off-white.

If one of the issues surrounding the question of commitment involves having a family together, then the energy of the north-west would be particularly helpful if your partner is male. If your partner is female, increase the chi energy of the south-west, which relates to motherhood. Do this by keeping yellow flowering plants in the south-west of your home and encouraging her to wear yellow clothes.

In addition, being more yang can help your lover to be more decisive. To surround your partner in more yang energy, give your home a good spring clean and try to keep the place generally neat and tidy: this will refresh the chi energy and allow it to move around more freely.

problem

I am in a happy live-in relationship, but my partner seems nervous about making a commitment. How can Feng Shui help me to resolve this dilemma?

just
common sense

If you are already in a happy relationship, ask yourself why you want your partner to commit further. If you are worried that he or she doesn't feel the same way as you or will leave when someone better comes along, it would be better to resolve these insecurities within yourself first.

If you are content within your relationship, it is likely that your partner will be too. Wear red and metal jewellery to absorb the more relaxing chi energy of the west.

water features

The presence of water is an important remedy in Feng Shui because the chi energy that is generated by water can influence the chi energy inside our bodies. Since 70 per cent of human body weight is made up of water, placing these features in your surroundings will have a significant effect on your personal chi energy.

Water features can be placed inside your home or out in the garden and come in many different shapes and forms. They range from outdoor waterfalls, garden ponds and bird baths, to indoor fountains, fish tanks or simply well-placed bowls of fresh, clean water. Many water features are available to buy in kit form, or you can make one yourself with a small water pump and an attractive display of rocks and pebbles in a large container.

YIN OR YANG?

Depending on the type you choose, water features can add either more yin or more yang chi energy to your surroundings. Features with fast-flowing water, such as fountains, will add more active yang chi energy to a room. Quick-moving fish in an aquarium will also create this kind of energy. Water features with still or slow-moving water generates more calming yin chi energy

Features with fast-flowing water have two practical advantages. The first is that because the water travels through the air, it collects dust and other particles and so helps to keep the surrounding air clean and fresh. The second is that running water produces a multi-frequency sound known as white noise. This masks other noises, such as the distracting background hum that you would be exposed to if you worked in an open-plan office or if you lived close to a main road.

To generate more calming yin energy, you will need to use a slow-moving water feature, such as some water gently trickling across

Water features that have air passing through the water are particularly good because the air oxygenates the water, keeping it fresh. Fountains and waterfalls create a similar effect.

a stone. Slow-moving fish in an aquarium, such as goldfish, will also create yin energy. If you do use an aquarium, line the bottom of the tank with real shells and pebbles (rather than plastic decorations), and consider growing some plants in the tank as well. These will help to prevent the water from stagnating or turning green.

THE PLACEMENT OF WATER FEATURES

Ideally, a water feature should be positioned in the east or south-east of your home. This way, the water energy nourishes the tree chi energy of the east and south-east. As the chi energy of the east is associated with ambition, confidence and activity, a water feature in this part of your home will bring out these aspects of your personality. A water feature in the south-east, on the other hand, will nourish the chi energy associated with communication, creativity and generating new ideas, helping you to move forward and build up your life.

If you place your water feature near a window so that the eastern sun touches it, this will further energize the water. A water feature will have a more yang influence if it is exposed to sunlight. As the sun is low in the east, it is often possible to site a water feature well away from the window, yet still find it receives direct sunlight. I place a bowl of fresh, clean water 7m from an eastern window, yet when I get up on a sunny day, the water is bathed in bright sunlight. Of all the Feng Shui solutions that I have introduced into my home, this has had the most immediate results: I am now more confident and ambitious, which has enabled me to expand my business.

Whatever type of water feature you choose, make sure the water is kept clean and unpolluted. If you are surrounded by stagnant water, its influence on the water chi energy in your body will be negative. The simplest way to refresh water is to take out a few mugfulls and refill with clean water. Another alternative would be to keep a bowl of fresh water in an appropriate place and change the water at the beginning of each day.

If a non-moving water feature, such as fresh water in a clear bowl, is placed in the path of sunlight, the water becomes energized and creates more yang energy.

An aquarium that has quick-moving fish generates more yang energy. However, one that has slow-moving fish generates more yin energy.

problem

I do not enjoy sex as often as my lover. The more frustrated my lover gets, the stronger the demands become and the more I recoil. How can Feng Shui help me to change this pattern of behaviour?

solution

As sexual activity is most likely to take place in the bedroom, you should concentrate your efforts in this part of your home. Ideally, the chi energy in the bedroom should be arousing and intimate for both you and your lover. To align yourselves with the chi energy that is associated with romance and pleasure, turn your bed so that the tops of your heads are pointing west. You can also try sleeping with the tops of your heads pointing in a northward direction because the chi energy of the north relates to sexual energy.

To increase the chi energy associated with sex, passion and romance, use the colours cream, purple, red or pink in your bedroom. Buy pure cotton, linen or silk sheets and bed clothes in these colours, and change them frequently to avoid exposure to stagnant chi energy. Fresh flowers are another way to introduce these beneficial colours into the room. Orchids are particularly good as they encourage sexual activity.

Candles create a more intimate light than electric lighting, so use lit candles in the bedroom. Pairs of candles or other paired objects, such as matching vases, are symbols of togetherness, so having these in your bedroom will also help to reinforce feelings of intimacy.

It may be that the chi energy in your bedroom is just not conducive to lovemaking, either because it is too cramped or there are sharp corners. If this is the case, experiment with other rooms in your home.

A healthy diet is important for sexual desire, so eat a good balance of foods. Too much fruit, wine or sugary yin foods can reduce vitality, while too much salt, meat, eggs or other yang foods can make you too tense.

just common sense

Discuss with your lover the possible reasons for your lack of enthusiasm. You may be too tired or stressed, or feel depressed or lethargic. Low self-esteem can also affect sexual vitality. Your lover may need to relax more about the issue to give you the space to do this. In the meantime, think about what your partner can do to help and work together to find a solution.

solution

If your new lover is too yang, he or she will be tense and serious, which makes it difficult to be uninhibited and adventurous about sex. If he or she is too yin, then your lover may simply lack the energy to do anything active and exciting. The Feng Shui solution to this problem, therefore, is to balance out personal chi energy.

If you think your lover is too yang, create a more yin environment by decorating your bedroom with cream or pale pink colours. Keeping candles and fresh cream flowers there will also help. Encourage your lover to cut down on eating yang foods such as meat, eggs and salt. Yang people often find it easier and quicker to relax after having an alcoholic drink, but I would not advise this as a long-term solution.

If you think your lover is too yin, you should consider preparing more yang meals that consist of seafood, root vegetables and grains: these foods will help to increase sexual vitality. You can also make the bedroom more yang by creating as much open space as possible. Choose decorative objects made from metal, stone and glass for your bedroom and, if there is a wooden floor, take up the carpets or rugs to expose it. Bright colours, especially reds, oranges and purples, will generate more yang energy, so have bed linen in these colours. Bear in mind, however, that a more yang bedroom can make it harder for you to fall asleep at night. If either of you are light sleepers, you may need to experiment with lovemaking in other rooms.

problem

I have met someone who is ideal for me in every way, except that our sex life is not very adventurous. Is there any way I can use Feng Shui to encourage my lover to be more courageous and exciting in bed?

If your lover is too yang, create a more yin atmosphere with lit candles and pale colours. This will foster a more adventurous attitude to sex. If your lover is too yin, boost his or her yang energy by displaying stone sculptures and preparing seafood dishes. This will increase sexual vitality.

problem

I am currently in a relationship, but recently have come very close to having an affair with someone at work. My resistance to temptation is very low. How can Feng Shui help to improve this situation?

solution

One of the problems in any relationship is that, after a while, complacency can set in. Once partners start taking each other for granted, resentment follows and the lure of an affair with someone who seems attentive and enthusiastic may be very strong. To prevent this from happening, focus your efforts on improving the quality of your existing relationship.

To regain feelings of intimacy with your partner, it would be helpful to increase the amount of south-western chi energy in your home. This can be achieved by placing yellow flowers in a clay container or charcoal in a clay pot and positioning them in the south-west of your home. Displaying family photographs in this area will also help to generate feelings of closeness. If you are a mother, sleeping with the top of your head pointing towards the south-west will be particularly helpful.

To recapture the romantic feelings you had when you first started seeing each other, increase your exposure to western chi energy. Position red or pink flowers, romantic pictures and any other pink decorative objects in the west of your home.

For a more positive outlook on your existing relationship, boost the amount of south-eastern energy in your home by placing a bowl of fresh, clean water, a tall plant and a mirror in the south-east of your home. If you are a father, sleeping with the top of your head pointing towards the south-east will be particularly helpful.

If you feel greater self-discipline will help you avoid having an affair, increase the energy of the north-west by placing a metal clock in this direction of your home.

You are most susceptible to having an affair when your Nine Ki year number is in the west, south-east or south.

One way to resist the temptation of an affair is to display photos of happy family occasions in the south-west of your home.

SOUTH-EAST
SOUTH
SOUTH-WEST
EAST
WEST
NORTH-EAST
NORTH
NORTH-WEST

solution

To recreate the sexual excitement that you once felt about your partner, try absorbing more of the chi energies of the north and west. The north relates to night and winter, a time for lovemaking and conception, and is also associated with the water element. Water chi energy promotes a powerful force that will help you and your partner regain more of the deeper, primal feelings of sexual desire for one another. The chi energy of the west relates to the end of the day and the sun setting, which is a time traditionally associated with romance. Once you have increased your exposure to northern and western chi, it will be easier to use conventional sexual aids, such as books, toys, games or videos, to revive this aspect of your relationship.

To expose yourself to more northern chi energy, decorate your bedroom with lots of cream colours. Make up your bed with cream-coloured linen and drape cream organdie or muslin over the headboard. You can also put cream lilies or orchids in a glass vase in the north part of your bedroom. If you like the sound of running water, keep a small fountain or another moving water feature in the east or south-east of your bedroom. This will help to boost tree chi energy in your room, encouraging you to be more active. To stimulate northern energy within yourselves, try sleeping in the north of your home or with the tops of your heads pointing in a northern direction.

To enhance the more romantic, western chi energy in your bedroom, keep a red or pink flower arrangement in the west of the room. You can also wear clothing with some red or pink in it. If you wish to create a more passionate atmosphere, place purple objects, such as flowers or candles, in the south of your bedroom. Lighting a candle in the south will also bring out more of this passionate energy. Pictures, paintings and sculptures that are sexually evocative will also increase sexual desire, so try putting these around your home.

It will be easiest to put more energy into your sex life when your Nine Ki year number is in the west, north or south.

problem

The sex in my long-term relationship has become repetitive and, to be honest, boring. How can I revive the passion and sparkle that once existed?

electromagnetic fields (EMFs)

Many of the tools used in Feng Shui are simple items or objects that are placed in appropriate directions of your home. However, one of the most important considerations for ensuring good Feng Shui is the flow of positive, healthy chi energy. One way of doing this is by reducing the level of harmful radiation in your home, and many of the solutions I advocate in this book to counter ill health and feelings of confusion and disorientation involve reducing your exposure to EMFs.

Anything that uses or transports electricity generates its own electromagnetic field (EMF). This includes computers, televisions, photocopiers, fax machines, electric blankets and heaters, mobile telephones, microwave ovens, electric cookers and hairdryers. These electromagnetic fields interfere with the surrounding chi energy and therefore your personal chi. Recent research from Montpellier University in France also suggests that exposure to EMFs increases the risk of fatigue, sore eyes, headaches, lack of concentration, irritability, backache and, more seriously, cancer.

REDUCING YOUR EXPOSURE TO EMFs

If you are planning to move home, make sure there are no electrical substations, high voltage power lines, power lines over railway tracks or industrial units that use a high voltage supply of electricity nearby. There is very little you can do to counter these outdoor EMFs and the closer you are to them, the greater the risk. As for indoor EMFs, the best way to reduce your exposure to these is to use electrical equipment and appliances only when you really need them. The reason for this is because the greater the use of electricity and the closer you are to the source, the greater the risk will be of your exposure to EMFs. When electrical equipment is not in

Research conducted by the Institut de Recherches en Géobiologie in Chardonne, Switzerland showed that the most effective plants for reducing headache and fatigue among Wall Street employees were cacti, peace lilies and spider plants.

use, make sure you unplug it from the electrical socket so that the electricity does not continue running through the transformer.

Try also to maintain a reasonable distance when using a computer or watching television. The most harmful EMFs are thought to extend 75cm from the front of a computer and television and 100cm from the rear. Often the greatest EMFs are generated by the transformer, so for equipment that has a remote transformer on a lead, such as a laptop computer, you should site the transformer well away from you, even though the screen and monitor of the computer are closer to you.

Growing healthy green plants is one Feng Shui solution to countering the harmful effects of EMFs. This is because the natural chi energy that plants generate helps to counter radiation. Keep as many plants as possible in the rooms of your home that have a television or computer. Fresh flowers also generate healthy chi energy, so keep these next to radios or stereos in kitchens and bedrooms.

You are at greatest risk from EMFs when you are asleep because you are dormant and passive in one place for a long period of time. To avoid this situation, arrange your bedroom so that electric alarm clocks, radios, other electrical equipment and power points are as far away from your bed as possible. You should also make your bed with sheets that are 100 per cent cotton as these help to prevent a static charge. Wearing lots of clothes made of natural fibres or having natural fabrics in your house in general will also surround you in healthy, natural chi, as will opening your windows and curtains to let in fresh air and natural light.

Your office is also likely to have many items that radiate EMFs so set up your desk area carefully to ensure electrical equipment is as far away from you as possible. A computer keyboard does not radiate significant EMFs so this can be kept close to you.

As well as plants, fresh air and natural light help to counter the effects of EMFs, so try to incorporate these elements into your home and office space.

An ordinary compass will indicate whether you are entering an EMF. Hold it in your hand, making sure the needle is steady, then walk towards an electrical item. If the needle changes direction, this indicates a disturbance in the earth's magnetic field, which results from EMFs.

problem

My husband and I are arguing a lot at home. Are there any Feng Shui recommendations that could help?

A home that is filled with pastel-coloured fabrics and wooden furniture will result in a more tranquil, yin atmosphere in which arguments are less likely to occur.

solution

If the atmosphere in your home is not very relaxing, then you will inevitably feel on edge and be more likely to argue with your spouse. To surround yourselves in a more tranquil environment, you should aim to make your home more yin.

Bright colours, such as red, orange, purple and yellow, are particularly stimulating yang colours, and overexposure to these could encourage confrontational behaviour. To activate more yin energy, you should therefore decorate your home with pale greens, blues, creams and other pastel colours instead. Flowers, fabrics and decorative objects are all good ways to introduce these colours into your home.

To create more slow-moving yin chi energy, have furniture in your home that is made from yin materials, such as wood and wicker. Glass, metal, marble and stone are all yang materials that will speed up the flow of chi energy, so avoid having furniture and surfaces made from these materials

Sharp, protruding corners also speed up chi energy. If the corners point to a place where you sleep or sit and relax, the fast-moving chi will affect your own energy field, making you feel more irritable. To help pacify fast-moving chi energy, place a plant with round or bushy leaves in front of these corners or drape some fabric over them.

Sleeping with the top of your head pointing south will expose you to a more active energy that could increase your tendency to argue and get annoyed with your partner. To align yourself with a more peaceful chi energy that, after time, can subtly calm your own chi energy, sleep with the top of your head pointing west, south-west, north-west or north. Sitting so that you face one of these directions while you relax in the evenings will also help.

If your front door is positioned to the south of the centre of your home or faces south, this will encourage more fiery southern chi energy to enter your home, bringing with it tension and arguments. To subdue this chi, paint your door matt black, brown, pale yellow or beige. You can also place yellow plants in clay pots on either side of the door – the soil chi energy associated with clay and the colour yellow will help to calm the destructive southern energy.

solution

According to Feng Shui, too much passion suggests an excess of the fiery southern chi energy in your home. This would most definitely be the case if your home faces south or its main entrance is to the south. To calm southern chi energy, you need to enhance south-western chi energy – the soil energy associated with the south-west will absorb some of the fire energy related to the south. South-western chi will also introduce more of the chi energy associated with being emotionally intimate and family oriented.

To boost south-western chi and calm southern chi, place yellow flowering plants in clay containers in the south and south-west of your home. Charcoal in clay pots placed in the south will also help, particularly if your home or its main entrance is facing south. Decorating the south of your home with objects and fabrics that are yellow, beige and matt black will help further.

To encourage your partner to participate in activities outside of the bedroom, try to increase the presence of south-eastern chi energy. The direction of this chi energy relates to the morning and spring, times associated with getting out and being active. To boost this energy, place a water feature and lots of tall plants in the south-east of your home.

If you feel you would both benefit from taking a more serious approach to your relationship, your should aim to boost the chi energy of the north-west. This can be achieved by keeping lots of silver, grey and off-white fabrics, furniture and decorative objects in this part of your home.

To immerse yourself more in any of the above energies, sit so you are facing that particular chi energy or sleep so that the top of your head is pointing in the related direction.

problem

Our relationship is based on lust and we seem to have little in common outside the bedroom. I am beginning to worry that our relationship has no future. How can Feng Shui help to bridge the gap?

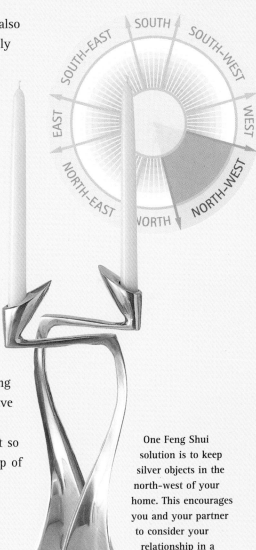

One Feng Shui solution is to keep silver objects in the north-west of your home. This encourages you and your partner to consider your relationship in a more serious light.

I love to be wined
and dined, given
presents and made
to feel special. Can
you please suggest
some ways to
encourage my lover
to be more romantic
with me?

solution

Your lover is more likely to make romantic gestures if the chi energy of the west is prominent in your home. This playful energy is associated with the youngest daughter, along with the end of the day and the setting sun, a time commonly associated with romance.

To build up more western energy in your home, decorate this area with fabrics and objects that are pink or red. Since pairs of items evoke feelings of intimacy, a good decorative feature to have in the west of your home would be a pair of red or pink roses in a metal vase. A mirror in the west of your home will also activate more western energy, but make sure that the back of it faces an outside wall.

To absorb more western chi energy at night, sleep so that the tops of your heads are pointing in this direction. You can also surround yourselves in more romantic energy by wearing pink and red clothes, and silver accessories and jewellery. Displaying romantic pictures, sculptures and poems in a prominent place will also help to encourage romantic feelings and actions. Try playing romantic music when you are relaxing together on the sofa or enjoying a dinner for two at home. Once you have created the appropriate atmosphere, you may need to show or explain to your lover the kind of romantic gestures you particularly enjoy because everyone has different preferences.

It would also help to make your home slightly more yin: if it is too yang, your partner may feel too rushed to make romantic or frivolous gestures. If there are long straight corridors or sharp corners and edges in your home, place some pot plants by these areas to calm the fast-flowing yang energy they generate.

Your lover will probably find it easiest to indulge your romantic notions when his or her Nine Ki year number is in the west, south-east, south or south-west.

To surround your lover in more romantic chi energy, play or listen to romantic music when eating dinner together. Displaying romantic pictures or sculptures in and around your home will also help.

solution

When there is a relationship between a more yin person and a more yang person, there is always a risk that the person who is more yang will dominate the person who is more yin. One solution to this problem, therefore, is to increase your exposure to more yang energy while increasing your partner's exposure to more yin energy.

To make yourself more yang, I suggest you try wearing more bright colours, silks, leather accessories and shiny metal jewellery. Hats, vertical stripes, high-heeled shoes and other items of clothing that create the illusion of increased stature will also help. Adopting a more formal appearance in general will make you appear more imposing to your partner, and you will feel more in control as a result. If you have your own space at home, such as a study or a walk-in dressing room, make this a more yang environment by decorating with bright colours and ensuring there are hard, clean and tidy surface areas.

Eating a diet that includes plenty of fish, root vegetables and thick soups will also help to boost your exposure to yang energy. Encouraging your lover to eat more yin foods, such as salads, fruit and leafy vegetables, will make him or her more relaxed, as will pursuing a relaxing activity such as t'ai chi or yoga. Once your lover absorbs more yin energy, you are less likely to feel so overwhelmed.

You will find you can regain your power most easily when your Nine Ki year number is in the north-west, north-east and east.

I find my lover overwhelming. At times I feel intimidated, at other times I feel pathetic and hopeless. I want to regain some of my power. How can Feng Shui help me do this?

Increasing your exposure to yang energy by wearing metal jewellery and bright colours will help you to regain some control in your relationship. At the same time, encourage your partner to eat more salads and do relaxing activities, such as yoga, to increase his or her yin energy.

problem

My partner and I both lead such hectic lives that we rarely see each other, let alone spend any quality time together. Can you recommend any Feng Shui solutions to this?

things
to avoid

The chi energies of the north-east and east can encourage you to devote more time to work, so avoid these by ensuring that your head is not pointing in these directions when you are asleep and you are not facing these directions when you are sitting down.

solution

If you both have demanding jobs and social lives, your home should be a real sanctuary where the two of you can unwind from the stresses of the outside world to focus on each other. To facilitate this aim, you need to create a relaxing yin ambience at home. You should also boost the chi energy of the south-west, which encourages you to be more settled and home-oriented, and the chi energy of the west, which helps you to feel more romantic and content.

To make your home more yin, soften any corners by placing bushy plants in front of them. If the corner of another building is pointing towards your home, you will be exposed to fast-moving, cutting chi, which can make it harder to feel settled. Placing a convex mirror or convex metal object, such as a plaque, outside your home where the corner is pointing, will reflect the sharp, cutting chi away from your home. A cosy atmosphere is more yin and this can be created by furnishing your home with large cushions and soft, comfy sofas and chairs. If you have wooden or stone floors, cover them with rugs as this will help to slow fast-moving yang energy.

Absorbing more south-western and western energy will help you to focus on your relationship and spend quality time together. To add more south-western chi to your home, keep clay pots or containers, natural fabrics and decorative objects made from soft stone in the south-west. Decorating the west and south-west parts of your home with yellow, matt black, pink and rusty red colours, as well as sleeping with the tops of your heads pointing in one of these directions will further help.

It will be easiest to spend quality time with your partner when both your Nine Ki year numbers are in the south-west, west, north or south-east.

solution

All these emotions that you are experiencing are symptoms of being too yang, so one Feng Shui solution to this problem would be to try and become more yin. The sharp, piercing energy of the north-east will also contribute to feeling tense, critical and short-tempered, so aim to reduce your exposure to this energy as well. At the same time, strengthening western or northern chi energy in your home will encourage you to be more relaxed in your relationship.

To make your home environment more yin, decorate with soft fabrics, pastel colours and plenty of plants that have floppy leaves. When you get home after work, change into loose, comfortable cotton clothes as these will encourage you to feel calm and content towards your lover. Eating a more yin diet that contains plenty of vegetables, fruit and liquids will also help you to relax, as will taking up t'ai chi, meditation or yoga.

To avoid absorbing north-eastern chi energy, turn your bed so that the top of your head is not pointing in this direction. If your home faces north-east or the front door is in the north-east, place a ramekin dish filled with one or two tablespoons of sea salt next to the front door or below the window. This will calm north-eastern chi energy. Bear in mind that it is good Feng Shui practice to balance this by placing another ramekin dish of sea salt in the south-west – the opposite direction – of your home.

To increase your exposure to the more romantic and fun-loving chi energy of the west, place pink flowers in a metal container in the west of your home. To boost the peaceful, flexible and affectionate chi energy of the north, you should put cream flowers in a glass container in the north. To absorb more of any one of these directions, you can also sleep so that your head is pointing in that particular direction.

You will find it most easy to resolve this problem when your Nine Ki year number is in the south-west, north or west. It may be hardest when your Nine Ki year number is in the north-east, east or south.

problem

I often feel tense with my lover, which results in me being critical and short-tempered. How can I be more relaxed in the relationship?

The chi energy of the north-east can make you tense and critical, so subdue this energy by placing a ramekin dish filled with sea salt in the north-east and south-east of your home.

problem

My lover has become extremely obsessive. I am on the verge of leaving but thought I would give it one last try with Feng Shui. Please advise me on what I should do.

solution

Obsessive behaviour is an indication of being too yang. It would therefore help if you encouraged your lover to absorb more yin energy. North-eastern chi energy can foster obsessive behaviour, so another Feng Shui remedy would be to decrease your lover's exposure to this energy, and build up the more playful chi energy of the west.

To surround your lover in a more yin environment, soften any sharp, protruding corners in your home by placing bushy plants in front of them. Similarly, trailing plants can be placed on top of tables with sharp corners. You can also position bushy plants along straight corridors or between several doors in a line. The plants will slow the flow of the fast, yang energy that is caused by long, straight lines.

You can also encourage your lover to become more yin by preparing yin meals that consist of raw vegetables, fruits and light dishes, such as stir-fried noodles. Yin pursuits, such as t'ai chi, yoga and meditation, will further help your lover by putting his or her mind at ease about you and the relationship.

To prevent your lover from absorbing the detrimental chi energy of the north-east, turn your bed so you and your lover are not sleeping with the tops of your heads pointing in this direction. To subdue north-eastern chi energy in your home, place ramekin dishes full of sea salt in the north-east and south-west parts of your home. Decorating the north-east of your home with the colours pink, off-white and light grey will help to calm the chi energy, as will placing round shapes and metal objects in this part of your home.

just common sense

Talk to your lover to see if there is a particular reason for these feelings of jealousy and obsessiveness. If you explain that you are feeling claustrophobic in the relationship, your lover may be willing to make changes in order to improve the situation. At the same time, you may discover aspects of your own behaviour that could be changed to help your lover feel less insecure.

Being more yin will help your lover become less obsessive, so encourage him or her to eat fruit and pursue relaxing activities, such as yoga. Also, soften any sharp corners in your home with trailing plants.

iron and metal

According to Eastern medicine, the level of iron in your blood has an impact on how determined, driven and strong-willed you are. Because the chi energy surrounding the iron particles in your blood is influenced by the chi energy of any iron in your environment, you can use iron objects to enhance or subdue these more yang character traits. Other magnetic metal objects that contain iron will affect your personal chi energy in the same way.

Iron and other metal objects are associated with the Five Element metal, which is associated with the chi energies of the west and north-west (see also page 41). As metal chi energy is related to round shapes, you can generate more metal chi energy by placing round metal objects – coins, plates, statues, pots and containers – in the west and north-west of your home. The more solid and heavy these objects are, the more yang they become. A heavy cast-iron container, for example, will be more yang than a collection of small coins.

All shiny metal objects, such as polished doorknobs and bathroom fittings, reflect chi energy regardless of the type of metal. These objects encourage chi energy to flow faster, which is good if you want to create a vibrant atmosphere. It will flow even more quickly if you keep these items in the west and north-west of your home.

Too much iron, however, can distort the earth's magnetic field (see also page 82–3). You should therefore avoid sleeping in an iron-framed bed, on a steel-sprung base or on a mattress with steel springs, as these all result in being exposed to a distorted magnetic field, which could increase the risk of you feeling confused and disoriented. Brass bedsteads, on the other hand, are not magnetic, so they will not have this effect.

One of the best ways to introduce more metal chi energy into your environment is by keeping a round clock with as many metal parts as possible in the west or north-west of your home. A pendulum clock is ideal because it also adds structure and rhythm to your life, making you more organized.

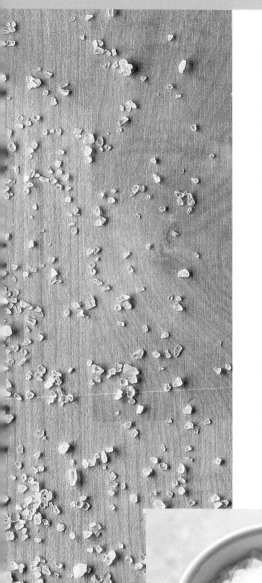

sea salt

Just like iron and water, salt is also found in our bodies, so having sea salt in your surroundings will influence your personal chi energy. Sea salt has a very yang quality and in the environment is related to the Five Element metal. It has the ability to draw in chi, so is particularly helpful for absorbing any negative chi energy, for instance, in a room where you have just had an argument with someone or when you move into a new home that may have bad chi from previous tenants. Sea salt is also a useful remedy for stabilizing chaotic chi energy.

To absorb negative chi energy, sprinkle pure sea salt on the floor in the area you want to cleanse before you go to bed. When you wake up, brush away or vacuum up the sea salt and immediately discard it outside your home. To stabilize chaotic chi energy, place sea salt near any windows or doors that are in the north-east and south-west of your home because these are areas that contain the potentially unstable soil chi energy. The salt does not need to be seen, so you can place it out of sight behind furniture. It is best to keep it on the floor, however, as this is more effective for something with yang chi energy.

If you have the option, it is best to obtain your sea salt from a health food shop as this will ensure that it generates the purest type of chi energy: sea salt stocked in supermarkets can sometimes contain additives, so if you purchase sea salt from the supermarket make sure you check the labels carefully. You should also endeavour to store sea salt in a dry place as this will help it to stay absorbent and therefore make it most effective.

Ideally, sea salt should be exposed to air, so I recommend putting one or two tablespoons of it in a ramekin dish and placing this on a window sill or directly on the floor.

solution

To avoid an inevitably unhappy situation, you might like to reconsider your decision to split up. Increased exposure to southern chi energy can increase your chances of becoming overly emotional, with the result that you may want to end a relationship. If you sleep with the top of your head pointing towards the south or your Nine Ki year number is in this direction, then the impulse to separate can be greater. If this is the case, move your bed to avoid absorbing southern energy when you sleep. Placing charcoal in a small clay pot in the south of your home will also help to subdue the effects of this energy. Try waiting until the following year when your Nine Ki number is no longer in the south, to see if you still feel the same way about your partner.

If, despite these actions, you are still determined to leave, absorb more south-eastern energy. The energy of this direction is associated with the wind and the traditional role of a caring eldest daughter, and it will encourage you to carry through your decision in a focused, but gentle manner. Adopting this approach should prevent any flare-ups or long-term pain and resentment. To increase south-eastern chi energy, place a calming yin water feature, such as a bowl of fresh water or water trickling over a stone, in this part of your home. Keeping tall plants here will further boost south-eastern chi energy, as will decorating with pale green and blue colours.

Making your home environment more yin may help because this chi energy encourages gentle, caring and considerate feelings. To do this, display cream-coloured flowers in more yin blue vases, and use pale green and blue fabrics around the home. If there are sharp corners or long corridors in your home, you can slow the fast-moving chi energy generated by these features by putting bushy plants in front of corners and along the corridors. Similarly, if you have stairs that lead straight to your front door or you can see the back door when you enter from the front door, you should break up this line of fast-flowing yang energy with lots of bushy plants. You should also avoid having mirrors that are positioned directly opposite a door window or another mirror, as this, too, will create fast-flowing yang energy.

problem

I have decided to end my live-in relationship, but would like to avoid causing any unnecessary pain. How can Feng Shui ease the situation?

More south-eastern energy can help you make the break in a considerate manner. To enhance this chi energy, put a bowl of fresh water and tall plants in the south-east of your home.

problem

I was very much in love with someone who fell in love with someone else. I feel terribly rejected and have lost my confidence and self-esteem. How can I get out of this rut?

solution

The end of a significant relationship often brings with it feelings of loss, be it of security, confidence or self-esteem, especially if your partner was the one who instigated the break-up. Nevertheless, you can boost your confidence by surrounding yourself in more eastern chi energy. This energy is associated with the dawn and springtime, so it is beneficial for getting out of the rut in which you have found yourself and for beginning a new phase in your life. At the same time, it would help if you surrounded yourself in more yang energy. This energy makes it easier for you to feel that the relationship break-up is your ex-partner's loss, and that a better relationship for you will result.

To increase eastern chi energy, place an indoor fountain and tall plants in the east of your home. Bright green colours will further help, so make sure any fabrics and decorative objects you have in this area, such as cushions or a vase, are green. Having wooden flooring, furniture and bench tops in your home will also boost the presence of eastern chi energy. To absorb more eastern energy at night, turn your bed so your head is pointing in this direction when you sleep.

Eating a more yang diet filled with fish, root vegetables and grains will help you to feel more enthusiastic about life, while engaging in competitive sports or martial arts will encourage you to be mentally strong. Regular body scrubs will encourage your personal chi energy to move faster, allowing you to let go of the disappointment and rejection you are feeling.

Keep your home clean, spacious and clutter-free to encourage chi energy to flow more freely. Undertaking a thorough spring clean of your home will refresh the surrounding chi energy and therefore encourage you to make a new start with your life.

FAMILY

4

problem

Our young baby is currently sleeping in our bedroom but we want to prepare a nursery for him. Is there anything we should be thinking about in terms of his well-being, before we begin work on the decor?

solution

The ideal atmosphere in a nursery is one that is conducive to the healthy development of a growing child – getting a good night's sleep in particular! The chi energies most beneficial to these aims are those of the east, south-east, west and north. The east symbolizes the beginning of a new day and your child's future; the south-east promotes growth and activity; the more settled western chi encourages peaceful sleep; and northern chi energy, the quietest energy of them all, is ideal if your child is having problems getting to sleep.

To absorb more of any of these energies, design the nursery so that the top of your child's head is pointing in one of these directions while asleep in bed. My own children sleep with their heads pointing eastward, although when they were younger and had difficulty getting

to sleep, I found that placing their beds so that their heads were pointing towards the west or north was more helpful. Given the space, children will often turn to a direction that most suits their needs at that time. If you observe the direction your child veers towards while asleep, you can discover which type of chi energy they need more.

To decorate the interior of the nursery, use light greens, pastel blues or pinks. These colours are associated with the east, south-east and west respectively, so will help to draw out the chi of these directions. Soft, pale colours will also help to create a more soothing atmosphere in general.

Make sure that curtains, bed linen and other fabrics you put in the nursery are made from 100 per cent cotton, linen, silk, wool or other natural materials. Cream colours and mottled patterns are particularly good for creating a calm, sleep-inducing atmosphere, so use where possible. Synthetic fabrics carry a static charge of electricity which can be disruptive to your child's personal chi energy, increasing the risk of tantrums and poor sleep, so you should avoid these.

solution

The Feng Shui solution to this problem would be to calm the more independent chi energy of the north and expose your family to more south-western chi energy. The south-west is associated with settling down and relates to the time when fruits ripen on the vine. The chi energy of this direction is therefore ideal for spending more enjoyable time together as a family.

To reduce the amount of northern chi energy in your home, keep plenty of tall plants, green-coloured fabrics and wooden furniture and decorative items in the north of your home. This will boost tree chi energy, which will help to drain the water chi energy associated with the north.

To enhance south-western chi energy, place some yellow flowers in a clay vase or a yellow flowering plant in a clay container in the south-west of your home. As yellow and matt black are the colours associated with the energy of the south-west, you should decorate your home in these colours wherever possible. A small amount of fire chi energy will nourish the soil chi energy of the south-west, so it will be useful to light purple candles in the south-west of your home as well.

Another way to increase your exposure to south-western chi energy is to sleep with the top of your head pointing in this direction or sit so you are facing this direction. If your home faces south-west or your main entrance is in the south-west, you will already be exposed to more of this chi energy.

problem

Over the years our family life has become fragmented with everyone doing his or her own thing. I miss the times when we used to play lots of games and go out together. What can I do to encourage the family to participate more as a group?

One Feng Shui remedy to this problem is to enhance the settled chi energy of the south-west by placing a yellow flowering plant in a clay pot in this direction of your home. Keeping lit candles in this area will further help to boost south-western chi energy.

problem

The television has become the focal point of our household. The children are obsessed with it and I am worried about the negative effects it could have on our health. What would improve this situation?

solution

Watching television is a relaxing pastime for many people. However, like most other electrical equipment, a television emits electromagnetic radiation. In Feng Shui, this upsets the orientation of the iron in your blood, particles of which align with the earth's magnetic field to give you a natural sense of direction. The effects of exposure to electromagnetic radiation are still being disputed by researchers but, in my opinion, exposure increases your risk of feeling disorientated and tired, as well as causing possible long-term health problems.

To limit your exposure, watch only the programmes in which you are interested and don't leave the television on for background sound. Unplug it once you have finished viewing so that electricity is no longer powering its transformer. As your personal chi energy is more vulnerable to outside influences while you are sleeping, be careful not to fall asleep with the television on.

The closer you are to a television, the greater the intensity of the electromagnetic fields (EMFs), so ensure that your children are watching from at least 2m away if it's a small television, and from 4m away if it is a larger one. To check the start of the EMF, hold a compass in your hand and walk towards your television. If the needle changes direction, you are moving into the field.

Healthy green plants add their own natural chi energy to an environment and will help to compensate for the effects of electromagnetic radiation, so place plenty of plants close to the television. Peace lilies, cacti and spider plants are considered the most effective against EMFs.

A more yang diet and lifestyle will encourage your children to play outdoors more.

To prevent your children's personal chi from being disturbed by the EMF caused by switched-on televisions, keep lots of plants nearby and use a compass to gauge how far away they should sit (see also pages 82–3).

solution

The chi energy of the north-west is associated with the fatherly qualities of leadership and being in control. Overexposure to this energy is most likely to make someone domineering, especially if that person is male. If your spouse is female, then an excess of south-western chi energy may also be the cause, as this energy is associated with the traditional role of mother. Your best chance of improving the situation, therefore, is by reducing the amount of north-western or south-western chi energy present in your home.

To reduce north-western chi energy, boost the energy of the north. The water chi energy associated with this direction will have a draining effect on the metal chi energy of the north-west. To increase northern energy, keep cream-coloured objects with a glossy finish in the north-west of your home. Glass items placed in this part of the home will further help, as will anything with curvy, flowing shapes such as glass sculptures.

If your spouse is female, add more metal chi as this will drain the soil chi associated with the south-west. To do this, decorate the south-west of your home with pink colours, round shapes and metal furniture or other metal items.

It would help to keep your home more calming, relaxed and yin in general, as this chi energy will counter the dictatorial nature of your spouse. To enhance yin chi energy in your home, use pale-coloured natural fabrics for curtains, rugs and bed linen, and grow plenty of plants with floppy leaves.

Do not sleep with the tops of your heads pointing north-west or south-west. More helpful directions are west, south-east or north. Similarly, this situation is more likely to improve when your Nine Ki year number is in one of these directions.

problem

My spouse is rather controlling and this takes all the fun out of everything we do as a family. This has worsened since we moved into our new home. How can Feng Shui help?

If your spouse is male, reduce the domineering fatherly chi of the north-west by putting a water feature in this direction of your home. If your spouse is female, decrease the motherly chi energy of the south-west by enhancing metal chi energy. This can be achieved by keeping pink flowers in a metal vase in the south-west of your home.

problem

To accommodate a growing family, we would like to add on a playroom and another bathroom to our home. What is the best Feng Shui way to do this?

solution

The first thing to consider is which directions are most suitable for these rooms. For a playroom, the north-east and west are good because these energies foster game playing and playfulness respectively. The south-east and east are also good because they both relate to the morning and springtime, which are symbolic for healthy childhood growth and development. The best location for a bathroom is in the east or south-east because the tree chi energy relating to these directions will be supported by the water chi energy of the bath, sink, shower and toilet.

In both areas you should use natural materials as much as possible. Wooden flooring is ideal for a room in the east or south-east of your home, as it is harmonious with the tree element related to the energies of these directions. However, make sure it is solid wood as a laminate wooden floor may release toxic fumes. Similarly, I would advise you to paint the walls of these rooms with natural, organic paint rather than lead-based paint.

If you want to create a relaxing atmosphere in the playroom, consider decorating the area with pale, yin-coloured fabrics and objects, such as greens, blues and creams. If you prefer to make the playroom more stimulating, bright greens, reds and yellows would be better. Having a mixture of direct and diffused lighting with separate controls is useful because this would allow you to make the atmosphere more yang or yin according to your children's ever-changing needs.

The ideal Feng Shui bathroom should be well-exposed to fresh air and daylight, whether it be through a window or skylight. These features will also enable you to grow lots of plants in the bathroom, which decreases the risk of damp, stagnant chi energy by absorbing excess moisture. Avoid fluorescent lighting because this creates a colder, blue-tinged light and emits more electromagnetic radiation.

To encourage the flow of healthy chi, both rooms should be decorated with organic paints and natural materials as much as possible. Depending on the atmosphere you want to create in the playroom, use soft lighting and pale yin colours to make it more relaxing, or spotlights and bright colours to make it more yang and stimulating.

solution

One way to reduce tension at the dinner table is to foster more calming yin energy. Another way is to increase your family's exposure to the chi energy of the north. This direction is associated with the night and winter, times that are considered quiet and peaceful.

To make the atmosphere of your dining room more yin, keep lots of soft, natural fabrics there. Good examples would be a pure linen tablecloth or large cotton napkins. If you can, opt for fabrics and other decorative items in pale blues, greens and creams as these are yin colours, which will further encourage relaxing energy.

If your table has sharp, angular corners, this will generate more yang energy. To counter this, keep bushy-leaved plants near the table. You can maintain a slow and steady flow of chi energy in the dining area by keeping the doors of the room closed while you eat.

Meals consisting of overly yang foods – meat, eggs and salt – mixed with yin spices and sugars, can heighten emotions and therefore increase the risk of tension. In general, it is better to feed your family a more balanced diet of vegetables, grains and salads, and to avoid preparing meals made from extremely yang foods. Replace sugary desserts with more healthy yin fresh fruit.

To increase your exposure to more northern chi energy, decorate the north-west, west, north, east or south-east of your home with cream colours, curvy shapes and glass objects. If one member of your family consistently seems tense, try seating him or her facing north. Other directions to face that will help make mealtimes tranquil and pleasant are west, north-west and south-west.

The chi energy of the south is passionate and potentially explosive. If your dining room is to the south of the centre of your home, your family will be exposed to more of this energy, which will aggravate your problem. To calm this energy, keep some charcoal in a clay container under your table and have pale yellow, beige or brown plates and other items in your dining room.

problem

Mealtimes in our house are filled with tension. My partner and I usually end up arguing with the children, then argue between ourselves about this. How can I make these occasions more peaceful?

problem

My children's table manners are atrocious and I am constantly nagging them at the dinner table. How can Feng Shui improve this situation?

solution

If you can create a more formal dining atmosphere that makes mealtimes dignified and serious occasions, it will be easier to impress upon your children the importance of good table manners. The metal chi energy of the north-west relates to fatherly control, self-discipline and dignity. It is the most formal of all the Eight Directions and is ideal for commanding greater respect from your children.

To introduce more north-western chi energy in your home, decorate this area with silver, grey and off-white colours. To make the table setting more formal, use adult crockery, shiny metal cutlery, and linen tablecloths and napkins. A solid, dark wood rectangular-shaped table with straight-backed solid chairs will generate more dignified chi energy in the room, encouraging your children to behave well. Lit candles on the dining table in a room will help to draw your children's focus to the meal and keep it there.

If you sit north-west from the centre so are facing south-east, you will be in the most powerful position at the table. This will help to ensure that your children respect your wishes to improve their eating habits. If your children are particularly unruly, place them at the table so they are facing north, west, north-west or south-west, because these directions surround them in more calming energy.

Extremely yin foods, especially those full of sugar, can raise blood sugar levels, making children hyperactive and unable to exercise any self-control. You should therefore try to cut out these foods from your children's diet. Some foods, such as baked beans, have 'hidden' added sugar, so check the ingredients list on food packaging carefully.

It will be easier for your children to behave the way you want them to when your Nine Ki year number is in the north-west, south-west or north-east.

solution

A settled, relaxed and more yin atmosphere is best for making the most of these family occasions. The chi energies of the west and north-west are also beneficial because they will encourage you to feel more relaxed and patient, and united as a family.

To make your dining room more yin, have comfortable wooden or wicker chairs to sit on and make sure there are large pastel-coloured napkins, flowers and a linen tablecloth on the table: these will all help to slow the flow of chi energy. If there are corners pointing at the table, place a bushy plant in front of them to slow the flow of chi. Avoid direct lighting by using up-lights, lampshades and candles instead. Changing into comfortable clothes before you eat, especially if you have been at work, will help to refresh your personal chi energy and make it easier to forget the stresses of the day and enjoy this time with your family.

To bring out more of the metal chi energies of the north and north-west, aim to keep rusty red, pink, grey, silver and off-white objects in the north and north-west of your kitchen and dining room. Pink flowers in a round, silver vase placed on the dining table would be ideal. Eating with silver cutlery will also generate more of these metal chi energies.

To absorb more west and north-western chi energy, sit down at the dining table so you are facing these directions. If this is not possible, try south-west or north because these directions generate a more calming chi energy. If possible, sit with your backs against the walls so you can all see the door and windows in the room.

Wicker and wood furniture, linen tablecloths and mats, large pastel-coloured napkins, and cream flowers will all help to create a more harmonious yin atmosphere in your dining room.

problem

Mealtimes are among the few occasions my spouse and I get a chance to catch up with our teenage children, who rarely spend any time at home these days. How can I ensure that these times are positive and harmonious?

just
common sense

If you have the time, consider preparing a meal with three or more courses. Provided this doesn't keep you in the kitchen, you will have more opportunity to stay at the table for longer and catch up on the news with your family.

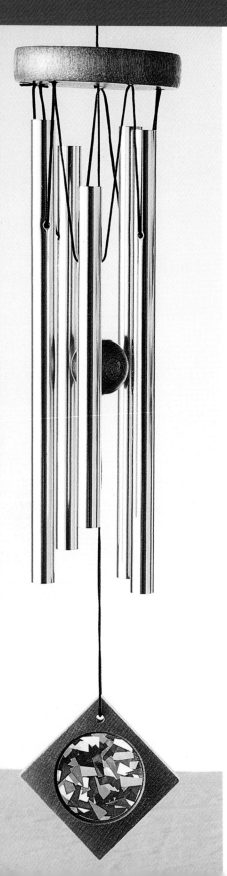

sounds

Sound travels in the form of invisible waves, which vibrate through the air. As these vibrations pass through your personal energy field, they activate or calm your chi energy, depending on the frequency of the sound wave. A soft, gentle sound is more yin, which helps to calm your chi energy, making you feel more relaxed. Vibrant, rhythmic sounds are more yang, activating your chi energy field to make you feel more energetic. This is why you may find yourself drawn to a serene piece of music when you are feeling tense and rhythmic dance music when you are feeling lethargic.

Chanting or singing is another way of using sound to adjust your personal chi energy. The sound waves you generate inside your body can vibrate your internal organs, effectively giving them an internal massage. Different sounds will have a greater influence on different parts of your body: a deep 'aah' sound will vibrate your lower ribcage, a higher 'ooo' sound will vibrate your chest, and a 'mmm' sound will vibrate the front of your skull.

In the same way that sounds can affect your personal energy field, household items that emit sounds – wind chimes, bells, clocks and moving indoor water features – can revitalize the quality of chi energy flowing through your home. This explains why metal bells, gongs and bowls are sometimes rung in monasteries, churches and places of spiritual worship: the vibrant energy of these sounds disperses negative chi and creates a cleaner, more spiritual atmosphere.

WIND CHIMES

These attractive decorations are particularly useful because, when hung by a door, they will send ripples of positive chi energy throughout the household every time you open the door. Wind chimes can be made from various materials, such as metal, wood or ceramic, and this will determines the type of sound they emit and in which direction it is best to keep them.

Sometimes wind chimes have light reflectors attached to them. Like crystals, these serve to disperse chi energy into different areas of a room, making these types of wind chimes extra powerful tools of Feng Shui.

Metal chimes, for example are most harmonious in the west and north-west because these directions are associated with the Five Element metal. However, they are also good to place in the south-west, centre and north-east of your home because these directions are all related to the Five Element soil, which is compatible with metal chi energy. Similarly, you can place a metal wind chime in the north of your home because this direction is related to the Five Element water, which is also compatible with metal chi energy. Placing metal wind chimes in a certain direction of your home will generate a more cleansing type of atmosphere there.

Wooden chimes are best in the east, south-east and south of your home because eastern chi energy relates to tree, which is compatible with the fire chi energies of the south and south-east. Wind chimes that are made of wood generate more positive and uplifting chi energy.

Ceramic wind chimes are good in the south-west and north-east because these directions relate to soil chi energy. They can also be kept in the south because this relates to fire, which is compatible with soil chi, and also in the north-west and west because these directions relate to metal chi energy, which is also compatible with soil energy.

BELLS

If you experience a heavy, stuffy or stagnant feeling in an area of your home, try ringing a resonating bell there. This can be particularly helpful when you have just had an argument or when you have finished tidying up after a party. If you have a large home, keep a large metal gong in the hall and hit it whenever you want to radiate cleansing chi energy throughout your home. For smaller spaces, you can buy metal bowls that ring when you hit them with a piece of wood.

Before you place in your home an object that emits a sound, make sure that you like the tone of it. I found the ring from modern telephones irritating, so in my home I keep the volume of these turned down and have added a telephone with a metal bell ring.

Place a telephone which has a metal bell ring in a corner of your home where the chi energy can be stagnant. Every time the telephone rings, the chi energy of that space will be activated by the pleasant-sounding metal ring.

Called singing bowls, these metal bowls are made from the following base metals: iron, lead, zinc, copper, silver and gold. They were traditionally used by Tibetan monks for meditation and healing.

problem

I get rather tense during big family occasions and would appreciate any tips on how to be more relaxed.

solution

There are a number of reasons why you may feel uptight in these situations. Once you have identified the cause, you can work out which type of chi energy will be most beneficial. For example, if you feel tense because you get nervous around people, expose yourself to more eastern chi energy as this will make you feel more confident and assertive. If you take on too much responsibility during these occasions, expose yourself to more north-western chi energy, which will encourage you to delegate and be more in control. If you just find the drama of these occasions too stressful, absorb more relaxing yin energy and the energy of the north, which helps you to be a little more detached.

The best way to address this problem is by changing your own energy field, rather than everyone else's. The easiest way to do this is by wearing clothes and accessories of certain shapes and colours. You don't need to dress yourself from head to toe in a particular colour and pattern – incorporating it into your overall outfit will be sufficient. To increase eastern tree chi energy, for example, choose something bright green or with a pattern of vertical stripes. Accessories made from wood will also help. To absorb more north-western chi energy, pick a grey or off-white piece of clothing from your wardrobe. Because the north-west is associated with metal chi energy, you can also wear round, metal accessories, such as silver jewellery. To absorb more northern chi energy, try cream-coloured or translucent clothing. A more flowing, curvaceous cut with lace or irregular patterns will also boost your exposure to northern chi energy.

To make yourself more yin and therefore more relaxed, try to eat plenty of vegetables, salads and fruit. At the same time, reduce the amount of meat, eggs and salty yang foods in your diet.

solution

Even the most united and harmonious of families can find Christmas a challenge and, although Feng Shui should not be used to paper over long-term family problems, it can help to improve the atmosphere for special occasions.

Generally, people will be more likely to argue with each other when they feel claustrophobic and cooped up. To avoid this kind of atmosphere, create as much space as possible in the rooms you are using. Clear away clutter and move any unnecessary furniture into another room. Open the windows and refresh the atmosphere. If things seem to be getting tense, suggest a walk outside.

To encourage lively, interesting and genial discussion, arrange chairs so that people are seated in a circle or oval. Avoid seating anyone so that they are close to a protruding corner or sharp edge: this places them in the path of fast-flowing, swirling chi energy, which can make them feel more ill-at-ease.

The energy associated with family harmony is most active in the south-west of your home. To foster this energy, grow a plant or keep an attractive fresh flower arrangement there. The colours yellow, matt black, brown or fawn are also helpful for encouraging this energy, so use these to decorate the south-west part of your home.

Sugary foods and alcohol can make people feel more impatient, irritable or short-tempered, so try not to consume too much of these, especially an hour or two after the big Christmas meal, which is considered the riskiest time for a family upset. To improve the balance of the meal, include plenty of steamed vegetables and salads. Radishes, mooli, vinegar, lemon and natural pickles will help to break down the fats contained in a traditional Christmas meal and ease the strain on your gallbladder and liver, so try to use these too.

problem

I always dread Christmas as it usually ends up being a stressful event with lots of arguments. Can I do anything differently this Christmas to help?

One way of ensuring family harmony is by boosting south-western chi energy. To do this, keep yellow flowers or other yellow objects in this part of your home. Sitting at a round dining table will also encourage lively, interesting and genial discussion.

problem

We're planning a birthday party for our five-year-old son. Is there anything I can do to ensure a good time will be had by all?

solution

A successful children's party is usually dependent upon its guests being outgoing enough to partake in games, but not becoming overexcited and prone to tantrums. The ideal environment for this would be one where the chi energy is more yang than yin, but not overly yang. It would also help to have a quieter, more yin area where shy or not-so-confident children can play with toys, listen to music or read picture books. A yin atmosphere is also best for cutting and distributing the birthday cake.

When your son's party guests arrive, usher them into the yang environment, which will encourage them to participate in games and activities. The yang area should be one of the larger rooms of your home that is fairly spacious and clutter-free. Move unnecessary furniture to another room, especially any soft, upholstered items because these generate more yin energy. Ideally, the yang area would have a polished wood or stone floor to allow chi to flow quickly, so take up any rugs and carpets. Coloured light bulbs in bright light fittings and colourful balloons will help to create a more stimulating, yang atmosphere, as will playing upbeat music. Mirrors and other shiny, reflective decorations will also help to make the room more yang. Open the windows regularly to allow fresh air into the room.

The more yin eating area should be decorated with soft materials, softer lighting and pastel colours. Large cushions on the floor or low, soft chairs will create a more secure and cosy atmosphere. Keeping leafy plants in this area will slow the flow of chi energy without causing it to stagnate.

just common sense

Foods containing lots of sugar can cause children to become hyperactive and lose self-control. It would therefore be better to serve savoury party snacks – mini pizzas, interestingly shaped pasta and vegetable kebabs – rather than sugary sweets and chocolate. Naturally sweet fruits like raisins or grapes, are more yin and will also help your young guests to relax. Serve sugar-free fruit juices instead of sugary soft drinks.

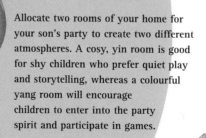

Allocate two rooms of your home for your son's party to create two different atmospheres. A cosy, yin room is good for shy children who prefer quiet play and storytelling, whereas a colourful yang room will encourage children to enter into the party spirit and participate in games.

solution

The type of party you want will determine the kind of restaurant to look for. If you hope to have a lively, exciting evening with lots of friends and relations who have not seen your parents for a while, then a restaurant with a more yang atmosphere will be conducive to this goal. If you are aiming for a relaxed, cosy gathering of immediate family, then choose a restaurant with a more yin setting because this energy fosters this type of atmosphere.

A yang restaurant will have lots of open spaces, big windows, bright lighting, a high ceiling and will be decorated with bright colours, such as as reds, purples and yellows. Polished wooden or stone floors, marble tables, large mirrors and shiny metal surfaces will encourage the pervading chi energy to move faster, which also makes for a yang environment. Shiny cutlery, sparkling glasses and bright flower arrangements are more yang features, which will also help to create a greater sense of occasion.

A more yin restaurant will be decorated with pastel colours like pale green, blue, pink and cream. The furnishings will be soft and upholstered, with tablecloths and large linen napkins on the tables. Diffused lighting, such as lit candles, wall lights or shaded table lamps, also creates yin energy.

Whichever atmosphere you choose, make sure that the table or tables in the restaurant are large and round or oval. This makes it easier for guests to interact. If it is practical, you should also aim to seat your parents at the north-west end of the table so they face south-east. This will allow them to absorb more of the north-western chi energy that is associated with leadership and respect.

patterns and shapes

The patterns that you find on wallpaper, curtains, cushions, upholstery, clothes or any other fabric can change the atmosphere of the surrounding space. This is because each type of pattern is either yin or yang and is associated with one of the Five Element chi energies, generating more of a certain type of chi energy in its surroundings.

The effect a pattern has on the atmosphere of a space tends to be quite subtle, but when it is used with colour (see pages 114–15), it can have a stronger influence. Combining a strong yang pattern and colour, for example, red and yellow diamonds, will make more of an impact on a room than a muted diamond pattern alone.

PATTERNS FOR SPECIFIC ROOMS

Because patterns affect your surrounding chi energy and therefore your moods, you should always make sure that any significant pattern you introduce to your home is appropriate to the kind of energy you want to generate in that particular room. For example, circular shapes foster the kind of energy that is associated with the end of the day, so this pattern would be good to have in a westerly dining room. You should also take the time to consider whether you can live long-term with more permanent patterns, such as those found on carpets or wallpaper, as you are unlikely to change these very often.

Vertical stripes add more tree chi energy to a space, making you feel more positive,

Thin, long, wavy patterns and shapes will generate more yin chi energy, whereas circular, octagonal, square patterns and shapes will create more yang chi energy. In general, having a busy, complicated pattern in a room will make the area feel smaller, whereas no pattern at all usually makes the space feel larger.

upbeat and better able to focus on your career. This pattern is therefore good to have in your study or office space. It is also a good pattern to have in an easterly or south-easterly kitchen, as it will help to create a a positive, healthy atmosphere. Vertical stripes also make a room appear taller, so this type of patterned wallpaper would be suitable for entrances, hallways, kitchens, bathrooms and small rooms as well.

Star shapes, zigzags or triangles are all patterns that add the Five Element fire chi energy to a room. This is an energy that encourages you to be more expressive, outgoing and sociable, and helps to create an atmosphere that is conducive to being active and busy. These types of patterns and shapes are therefore suitable for decorating rooms in which you socialize or interact with others, such as the living room.

Horizontal lines or long horizontal, rectangular shapes enhance soil chi energy, which makes it easier to feel more settled, intimate and comfortable. A room with lots of horizontal lines in the decor will seem cosier because the ceiling will appear lower. This pattern is therefore good to have in living or family rooms.

A wallpaper pattern consisting of round shapes will increase the Five Element metal chi energy, which helps you to feel more content and to focus better on end results. A room with lots of circular patterns will feel whole and complete, rather like the feeling you hope to have at the end of a day. This type of pattern is therefore good to have in your study, dining room or bedroom.

A wavy, mottled or irregular pattern will increase water chi energy, which helps you to be relaxed, feel more at peace with the world and act spontaneously. Sponging, rag-rolling or brushing the walls of a room are all techniques that create irregular patterns. Incorporating creams, blues and greens into a room with wavy or mottled shapes will accentuate this calming effect even more.

Irregular or unusual patterns are most suitable for bedrooms. A pattern that is ordered and repeats itself often is more yang. If you have pictorial patterns in your home, such as floral wallpaper or stars and moons, the images should have positive connotations for you. Repeated patterns are best used in more yang, open areas, such as hallways.

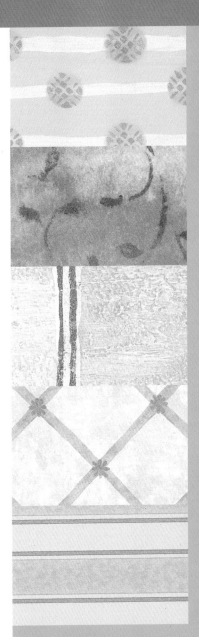

Each Five Element relates to a shape: metal to round, domed and arched shapes; water to irregular, wavy or mottled ones; tree to tall, thin and vertical shapes; fire to pointed, star, serrated, triangular, pyramid, diamond or zigzag ones; and soil to wide, checked or horizontal ones.

problem

My parents and my spouse's parents are frequent visitors to our home. I know they want to spend time with their grandchildren, but their visits are often stressful and tiring. How can Feng Shui help this situation?

solution

To be more organized and better able to plan ahead, immerse yourself in the metal chi energy of the north-west. This energy also encourages you to feel more in control of situations, which will prevent you from getting tired and feeling stressed around your frequent visitors.

To surround yourself in more north-western chi energy, decorate the north-west of your home with grey and silver colours. A round pendulum clock with metal parts, or any other solid metal object placed in this part of your home will also bring out more of this beneficial energy. When you arrange the visits, try sitting so you face north-west. Similarly, when your parents and your spouse's parents arrive, position yourself in the north-west of the reception room so you face south-east. This will help you feel more in control and able to delegate.

Another solution would be to cultivate more south-western soil chi energy in your home. This energy helps to create an atmosphere that is conducive to everyone enjoying family get-togethers. To generate more of this chi energy, decorate the south-west of your home with yellow, beige and brown objects. Putting yellow flowers in a clay container, charcoal in a clay pot or spreading plants in the south-west of your home will further enhance the chi energy of this direction.

Becoming more yin will help you to relax generally during family gatherings, so adapt your diet to include more raw vegetables, fruit, salads and other yin foods. As a more long-term approach, consider taking up yoga, t'ai chi or another meditative and reflective pastime. These yin-generating activities will make it easier for you to overcome potentially stressful situations.

Enhancing north-western metal chi energy will help to prevent you from getting stressed and tired around your visitors. Generating more south-western soil chi energy will further help by creating a happy and enjoyable family atmosphere.

problem

My mother-in-law lives with us. She is rather domineering, and her presence in the home is putting a strain on my marriage. How can I use Feng Shui to ease this situation?

solution

Although I would not suggest that Feng Shui alone can solve this type of problem, you may be able to influence your chi energy and that of your mother-in-law in a way that helps your predicament.

To assert your own energy within your home, make sure you sleep and sit in places that give you greater self-esteem and confidence. One way to do this is to sit in the corner of a room, furthest from, and facing, the door. If you have a choice of bedrooms, make yours the one in the east, south-east or north-west part of your home as these directions all encourage confidence. If your bedroom is not in any of these directions, turn your bed so that the top of your head is pointing in one of these directions.

To encourage your mother-in-law to feel more content and relaxed around you, make sure that she sleeps in the north or west of your home, with the top of her head pointing in one of these directions. Similarly, when you are sitting down together at family occasions, seat your mother-in-law so that she is facing north or west – directions that are associated with tranquillity and contentment respectively.

Use peaceful colours, such as cream, pale green or a pastel shade of blue, to decorate your mother-in-law's bedroom. To foster a relaxed and calm atmosphere in her bedroom, keep a plant with large floppy leaves, such as a cheese or rubber plant, there. Meanwhile, surround yourself with vibrant, upward-growing plants, such as ferns, palms and peace lilies. These will help to build up your own chi energy.

To reinforce your prominence in the household, display photographs and other reminders of yourself in a family role around the home. To strengthen your chi energy as the mother, place yellow flowers, or a yellow flowering plant in a clay container, in the south-west corner of your home.

To appear more assertive, try wearing bright green, purple or red clothes. Vertical stripes and fitted garments can make you appear taller, so wear these to discourage your mother-in-law from dominating you. Silver or gold jewellery will increase the chi energy associated with dignity, so wear this to encourage your mother-in-law to respect your position in the family.

One way to improve this situation is to wear gold or silver jewellery. This will generate an air of dignity and will encourage your mother-in-law to respect your position in the household.

colours

The colours with which you choose to decorate your home can have a significant effect on the surrounding chi energy. This is because light that is directed onto coloured walls or objects results in different light frequencies reflecting back out into your personal energy field, which then affect your emotions and thoughts.

Each of the Eight Directions is also associated with a specific colour. Putting a particular colour in the corresponding direction of your home or a room can strengthen the chi energy of that direction. The chi energy of the south, for example, generates expressive emotions and sociability. It is also associated with the colour purple. If you want to become more outgoing, decorate the south of your home with bright purple objects to strengthen this beneficial chi energy. To discover the colours associated with each direction and personal characteristics, refer to the chart opposite. The Japanese Nine Ki colours used here differ from the Five Element colours.

As well as being used to paint walls, ceilings and floors, colours can be introduced into a space by way of fresh flowers, plants, furniture, fabrics, pictures, works of art, and decorative objects and ornaments. The stronger and brighter the colour, the less you need to have for it to be effective. A small red cushion, for example, will have as much impact on a space as a soft pale pink sofa or wall. To get the balance right, you need to consider the hue and the area you are intending to colour.

SUBSTITUTING COLOURS

Sometimes, you may have a particular aversion to a colour, in which case you can substitute it for another. Using the principles of the Five Elements (see pages 30–1) you can interchange colours that are related to directions with the same Five Element. Matt black, for example, is the colour associated with the chi energy of the south-west. If you feel black

Colours are one of the easiest tools of Feng Shui because they can be introduced into your home in a variety of ways. Flowers are a particularly good way because they also introduce live, healthy chi energy into a space.

North	North-east	East	South-east	South	South-west	West	North-west	Centre
Cream, translucent or glossy	Bright white	Bright green	Blue or dark green	Bright purple	Matt black	Pink or rusty red	Silver, grey or off-white	Yellow
Independent	Motivated	Ambitious	Emotional	Settled	Romantic	Self-controlled	Powerful
Objective	Competitive	Confident	Creative	Expressive	Stable	Goal-oriented	Dignified	Attention-seeking
Sexual	Quick-witted	High self-esteem	Imaginative	Passionate	Quality-driven	Financially aware	Responsible	Opportunistic
Relaxed	Sharp	Energetic	Persistent	Sociable	Practical	Playful	Organized	Changeable
Spiritual	Wise	Enthusiastic	Sensitive	Quick-thinking	Realistic		Wise	
					Intimate			

is too oppressive a colour to use in your home, you can replace it with yellow or white, the colours associated with the chi energies of the centre and north-east respectively. This is because all three of these directions are related to the Five Element soil.

Similarly, green can be substituted for sky blue because the directions with which these colours are associated (east and south-east respectively) are both related to the Five Element tree. Red, pink, grey, silver and off-white are also interchangeable colours because the directions they relate to (west and north-west) share the same Five Element metal. Bear in mind, however, that cream and purple cannot be substituted for other colours because their Five Elements (water and fire respectively) relate to one direction only.

Using the principles of the Five Elements, colours can support or calm the chi energies of other directions: east and south-east are supported by cream and calmed by pale purple; south is supported by green and sky blue, and calmed by pale yellow; south-west, north-east and centre are supported by bright purple and calmed by grey or pink; west and north-west are supported by bright yellow and calmed by cream; and north is supported by red and calmed by pale green or blue.

Since the chi energy of each direction is related to a certain colour, you can choose specific colour schemes to help create the most appropriate type of chi energy in a room. For example, green and blue are good for a kitchen to the south-east.

problem

My spouse worries about our children to the point where they are prevented from doing things. This attitude is rubbing off on the children, who are now becoming fearful themselves. How can Feng Shui change this?

solution

In Feng Shui, worry is associated with the water chi energy of the north. If your spouse has always been cautious and anxious, it may be difficult to change this way of thinking. However, if he or she wants to adopt a different attitude to your children and is keen to try Feng Shui, then reduce the amount of northern water chi energy in your home. Since the tree chi energy of the east calms water chi energy, aim to increase this energy in your home as well.

If your home faces north or its front door is to the north, there will already be an abundance of northern chi energy in your home. To calm this excess, paint your front door green. This colour is associated with tree chi energy, which calms water chi energy. Hanging a wooden wind chime inside your door will also help, as will placing healthy plants and other green or wooden objects by the front of your home.

To reduce your exposure to northern chi energy at night, make sure your spouse is not sleeping with the top of his or her head pointing north. Similarly, he or she should not be facing this direction when sitting down to eat or relaxing on the sofa during the day. Sleeping with his or her head pointing east and sitting so he or she is facing this direction will drain water chi energy and encourage your spouse to be more confident, adventurous and positive. To further boost eastern tree chi energy, place a moving water feature, tall plants and bright green-coloured fabrics and decorative items in the east of your home.

To avoid an excess of water chi energy in the north of your home, keep tall plants in this area. If your bathroom is in this direction, there is a greater risk of dampness, which can cause negative, stagnant chi. To counter this, make sure your bathroom is kept well aired, dry and as clutter-free as possible. Keeping plants here will absorb excess moisture, but you may need to experiment with plants that require little sunlight, such as ivy.

A year when your spouse's Nine Ki year number is in the north will be a difficult time to break the habit of worrying about your children. The easiest time will be when your spouse's Nine Ki year number is in the east, south-east or west.

solution

If your husband is eager to spend more time with your children, the greatest encouragement he can receive is to enjoy the time he presently spends with them. To help him have more fun with the children, generate more of the playful and youthful western chi energy in your home. You can also increase the presence of the settled south-western chi energy as this traditionally relates to the mother-figure and will encourage him to feel more caring, sympathetic and family-oriented.

To immerse your husband in more western energy, move your bed so that the top of his head is pointing west when he sleeps. Encouraging him to sit facing this direction at the dinner table or when he is relaxing in the living room will also help. Red and pink are the colours associated with western chi energy, so having red or pink curtains, throws, cushions and other fabrics in this direction of your home will also generate more western chi energy. Flowers are another good way to introduce these colours into this area. Keeping metal sculptures, a money plant, board games and toys that both your husband and children enjoy in this part of your home will further boost western chi energy.

If you feel that the motherly chi energy of the south-west would be more beneficial to your husband's relationship with the children, turn your bed so the top of your husband's head is pointing in this direction when he is asleep. You can also keep yellow flowers in a clay vase, charcoal in a clay container and lit candles in this part of your home to boost south-western chi energy. Displaying family photographs and your children's paintings, drawings and other artistic creations in the south-west will also help.

Your husband is likely to spend more time with his children when his Nine Ki year number is in the south-west, west or south-east.

problem

I am worried that my husband rarely sees our children. They are asleep when he comes home from work and he is either too busy or too tired at the weekends to play with them. How can Feng Shui help to change this?

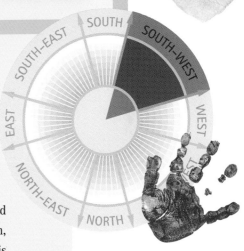

Displaying family photographs and your children's artworks in the south-west of your home is one way to boost the more family-oriented chi energy of this direction.

problem

Recently my wife has been feeling tense and irritable, and is nagging the children as a result. I am worried that this is driving them away. What can I do to prevent this?

solution

People who tend to impose their will on others are usually too yang. Being in an overly yang environment can also make a person feel tense. If your wife wants to be more relaxed with the children, it would therefore help if she became more yin.

An excess of north-western chi energy can make a person more prone to organizing others because the chi of this direction relates to the fatherly characteristics of leadership and being in control. Reducing the amount of north-western chi energy in your home and enhancing the chi energies of the west, north and south-east, which encourage playfulness, peace and positivity respectively, will further help.

To surround your wife in more yin energy, decorate your home with pale blues, greens and creams. Soft furnishings are also relatively yin, so keep lots of comfortable cushions and large upholstered chairs and sofas in your living room. Encouraging your wife to eat lots of vegetables, salads and fruit, and to take up a relaxing hobby such as yoga, t'ai chi or meditation, will also make her more yin in the long term.

To reduce your wife's exposure to north-western chi energy, turn your bed so she is not sleeping with the top of her head pointing in this direction. Since metal is the element related to the north-west, it is worth trying to limit the amount of metal furniture, surfaces and decorative objects made from metal in your home. Keeping cream-coloured and curvy-shaped objects in the north-west of your home will help to decrease your wife's exposure to north-western chi energy.

To increase the beneficial chi energy of the west, keep red or pink flowers in a glass vase in rooms that are in the west of your home. To boost northern chi energy, hang a crystal from the ceiling in this direction of your home. Lastly, to enhance south-eastern chi energy, you should place a still water feature in this part of your home.

solution

Your children are more likely to fight with each other if they are restless, frustrated and bored. To help them feel content, direct their energies towards something constructive. If your children only fight at home or in one particular room of your home, then try making changes to your home or the room to create a more tranquil atmosphere.

If your children's playroom is in the north-east of your home, your children will be exposed to a competitive energy that is likely to encourage tantrums and make them less willing to share their toys. To subdue and stabilize this energy, place small, white ceramic bowls filled with two tablespoons of sea salt in the north-east and south-west of the playroom. Decorating with the colours pink and grey will also help to subdue the aggressive energy generated by the north-east. The ideal direction for a playroom is in the west, east or south-east of your home.

To promote a more calming atmosphere, paint the walls of your children's playroom pale green or blue, and use pastel colours in general to decorate the room. Avoid keeping fiery red or bright purple objects in the room as these are more aggressive, yang colours that increase the risk of aggressive behaviour. Dress your children in pure cotton or other natural materials because these don't carry an irritating static charge, unlike synthetic materials. If you sense that your children are becoming agitated and restless, open the windows to let in some fresh air.

Plenty of indoor plants will add a more natural energy to the room, which helps to reduce the risk of feeling cooped up. Different types of plants will have different influences, depending on the shapes of their leaves and flowers, so experiment to see what helps your children. Plants with floppy round-shaped leaves are more calming, so these are preferable to plants with sharp edges, which can make the atmosphere less relaxing.

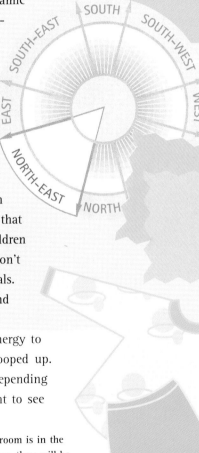

If your children's playroom is in the north-east of your home, they will be exposed to aggressive and competitive chi energy. To subdue this, decorate this direction of the room with pale pinks and greys. It will also help to dress your children in pastel-coloured clothes made from natural fabrics.

problem

My children spend a lot of their time fighting. They fight over their toys and argue during games they play together. What can I do to encourage them to get on better?

problem

My baby wakes up crying several times in the night and my older children, who previously slept through the night, are now waking up and coming into our bed. What will help us all sleep better?

solution

One reason for children not being able to fall sleep is because their energy levels are too high and their minds are still very active. The Feng Shui remedy is to move your children's chi energy down and away from their heads around bedtime. Submersing your children in a more yin environment just before they go to bed will also help to quicten their mental activity and allow them to fall asleep more easily.

One way to move chi energy away from the head and towards the feet is to put your children in a hot bath just before bedtime. Adding one or two drops of a calming aromatherapy oil to the bath will further help to relax them enough for sleep. Bathing by candlelight rather than electric light will add to the soothing atmosphere and will also be an enchanting change for your children. Make sure that the candles are out of their reach and well-secured to prevent any accidents.

To generate more calming yin energy in your children's bedrooms, ensure that the colour scheme incorporates pale green, blue and cream. Since synthetic bed linen emits an electromagnetic charge and can reduce your children's ability to relax, I suggest using 100 per cent cotton sheets along with a feather- or silk-filled duvet. Wood is a relatively yin material, so a wooden, slatted bed is preferable to a metal frame or a bed with metal springs. To align your children with more peaceful chi energy, reposition their beds so that the tops of their heads are pointing north, north-west or west.

things to avoid

Don't give your children sugary foods or allow them to watch dramatic or frightening television programmes just before bedtime. These can increase their mental activity, making it harder for them to relax and fall into a deep sleep.

solution

Being a bit more yang will encourage your children to concentrate better, develop organizational skills and generally take their studies more seriously. If they become too yang, however, they may become restless and yearn to go out instead. It is therefore important that you get the correct balance.

One way of ensuring that your children absorb the appropriate level of yang chi energy is to make sure that they keep their desks clean and relatively clutter-free. If they are working in cramped or messy conditions, their ability to be productive will be stifled. Wooden floorboards in their rooms and wooden desks or other smooth surfaces will help to ensure that chi energy moves smoothly.

The direction your children face when sitting at their desks will expose them to different types of chi energy that are supportive in different ways: facing east will encourage them to become more focused, precise and enthusiastic about studying; facing south-east will foster greater creativity, imagination and persistence; facing south will help your children to develop quick-thinking skills and greater pride in their work; facing south-west will boost their practical research skills and their ability to produce more quality work; facing west will surround them in an energy that allows them to enjoy their work and complete projects more easily; facing north-west will allow them to be more organized, serious and responsible; facing north will help them to become more independent and develop original ideas; and finally, facing north-east will surround them in an energy that encourages them to be competitive and hard working.

Once you have identified which energy would be most helpful to your children's individual needs, you can then move their desks so that they are facing this direction, and therefore absorbing more of this energy, while they work.

problem

My teenagers are not doing very well at school. How can I set up their study area to encourage them to make strides with their school work?

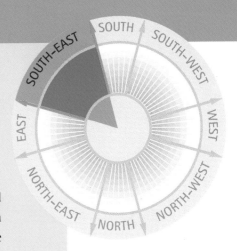

Facing south-east is just one of the useful directions to seat your children at their desks. This chi energy boosts their creativity and persistence.

problem

My children are very untidy and leave their clothes and books all around the house. What can I do to teach them to look after their belongings better?

just
common sense

By setting an example in the rest of your home, your children will learn how to be more tidy. Also, make sure they have lots of cupboards, shelves and other storage space in their bedrooms so they have somewhere to put their belongings.

solution

The most helpful chi energies for developing a sense of tidiness are those of the north-west and north-east. The north-west relates to organization, self-discipline and feeling in control, while the north-east is a clean energy that is associated with being sharp and precise. If your children can absorb slightly more of these chi energies, they will develop a more organized attitude to their own space. Being slightly more yang will also help because people with this energy are more likely to feel uncomfortable living in a messy environment.

To increase your children's exposure to north-western chi energy, keep round clocks with as many metal parts as possible – a pendulum clock is ideal – in the north-west of their rooms. You can also decorate this area of their rooms with metal, grey and silver-coloured fabrics and objects, as well as round shapes.

To enhance the presence of north-eastern chi energy, place white crystal rocks in this direction of your children's rooms. Keeping lots of white colours, horizontal shapes and objects made from stone in the north-east their rooms will also foster this beneficial chi energy.

You can also turn their beds so that the tops of their heads are pointing towards the north-west or north-east when they sleep, or rearrange their desks so that they face one of these directions when they are studying.

To encourage your children to develop more personal yang energy, prepare thick vegetable soups, hot fish casseroles and other meals that consist of yang foods. Try to eliminate sugary foods, such as soft drinks, sweets and ice creams, from their diets as these generate more yin energy.

One way to encourage your children to be more tidy is by enhancing their exposure to more chi energy of the north-west. You can do this by placing round, metal objects, such as a metal pendulum clock, in the north-west of your home.

solution

Generally, being timid and easily upset is a sign that your children are too yin. To help them become more confident and expressive, you need to enhance their yang energy. To do this, change their diet so they eat more thick soups, stews and grains, such as brown rice and porridge. At the same time, reduce their intake of yin foods such as raw, cold and sugary foods, including soft drinks.

In addition to changes in diet, you can change your children's surroundings so that they are exposed to more yang energy by making sure they have plenty of open space. Limit the clutter in their bedrooms and encourage them to go outdoors into the fresh air every day. Vigorous exercise will activate them, with the result that you may notice they are more talkative afterwards. Bright colours, shiny objects and plenty of light will also help to achieve a more yang atmosphere.

The chi energies of the east, north-east and south are related to confidence, motivation and being expressive respectively. To increase the presence of any of these within your child's own chi energy field, position your children's beds so that they sleep with the top of their heads pointing in one of these directions.

There are also ways to increase one or more of these energies within your home. To build up the chi energy of the east, position a flowing water feature, such as a small fountain, in the eastern part of your home or use green-coloured objects when decorating. Tall, leafy green plants and wooden furniture and surfaces are ideal for increasing eastern chi energy. They also encourage chi energy to move around faster than rugs or carpets.

To increase north-eastern chi energy, use bright white colours when decorating. Surfaces that are made of tiles or stone will also boost this energy and encourage a faster, more yang flow of energy.

To increase southern chi energy, use the colour purple, bright lights and pointy-shaped objects, such as star-shaped candleholders. Plants with pointed leaves, such as palms or yuccas, are particularly effective when placed in the southern part of your home.

To help your children become more yang and confident, decorate their bedrooms in bright colours, expose them to fresh air and lots of light and encourage them to eat warm stews.

problem

My children seem hyperactive; they are noisy and cannot settle down. They have difficulty completing their homework and, consequently, are not doing as well as expected at school. How can Feng Shui help?

solution

Yang energy can make a person feel restless. Being hyperactive, therefore, is a sign that your children are too yang. To remedy this, surround them in more yin energy. Enhancing the chi energies of the south-west, west, north-west and north may help your children complete their homework because these energies are all related to times when the sun is moving down, creating more settled chi energy.

To make your children's surroundings more yin, keep lots of pale green, blue, pink and cream-coloured fabrics and decorative objects in their bedrooms. Children usually love sitting on large cushions and beanbags, so scatter a few about their play area or bedrooms. These and other soft furnishings, such as rugs and curtains, will create a beneficial yin atmosphere. Encouraging them to wear clothes in these colours will also help to immerse them in more yin energy.

If there are prominent mirrors in your children's bedrooms, the chi energy will spin around more quickly, generating a faster, more yang type of energy that can make it harder to feel calm and relaxed. It would be a good idea, therefore, to remove the mirrors from their bedrooms for a while. Similarly, protruding corners caused by wardrobes and desks will cause fast-moving chi energy, so place a bushy plant in front of any such corners to slow the flow of chi.

To immerse your children in the beneficial south-western, western, north-western or northern chi energies, reposition their beds so that their heads are pointing in any of these directions when they sleep. It will also help if they sit facing one of these directions while doing their homework. Make sure that their desks are clean and tidy as this will allow chi energy to flow more smoothly.

To generate more calming yin energy, have indirect lighting and pale colours in your children's bedrooms and play areas. Keeping lots of large cushions and soft fabrics there will also help.

solution

By keeping the environment and routine in both homes as similar as possible, your children will experience consistency, which will encourage feelings of stability and security. To achieve this, arrange with your ex-husband to set the same bedtimes and mealtimes so your children can enjoy a daily rhythm regardless of where they are. It would also help if you kept similar decorations in their bedrooms, such as the same patterned bed linen or toys, as this will reassure them as they move from one home to the other.

problem

My husband and I are divorced and our children spend equal time with each of us in our respective homes. Is there anything I can do to help them feel stable and secure?

Some Feng Shui solutions to this problem would be to increase your children's exposure to the chi energies of the east and south-west. Eastern chi energy will encourage your children to feel confident and positive about their living situation, while the chi energy of the south-west will make them feel more secure and stable.

To immerse your children in more eastern chi energy, choose green fabrics and objects in which to decorate their bedrooms and keep lots of healthy plants there. Placing a water feature, such as a fish tank, in the eastern part of their bedrooms will also help to boost this energy.

To increase your children's exposure to the secure chi energy of the south-west, I suggest you place some charcoal pieces in a clay pot and keep this in the south-west of their bedrooms. Putting one or two tablespoons of sea salt in a ramekin dish and placing this in the south-west and north-east of your children's bedrooms will further help to stabilize south-western chi energy and make your children feel more secure about their living arrangements.

problem

To make your daughter more passive and yin, prepare lots of fruit and vegetables for her to eat. Decorating her room with pastel colours will also help, as will encouraging her to play quietly on her own.

solution

In Feng Shui, a desire to take control suggests a more yang nature, as well as an abundance of north-western chi energy. The north-west relates to qualities associated with the traditional father-figure, such as organization and leadership. Although the chi of this direction is useful in an adult, it is too mature an energy for a child. To discourage your daughter's bossy nature, you should therefore aim to decrease her exposure to north-western chi energy and try to make her more yin.

If your daughter is sleeping with her head pointing towards the north-west or her bedroom is in the north-west of your home, she will be absorbing this energy at night. You can rectify this situation by swapping bedrooms (in Feng Shui tradition, a bedroom in the north-west should be occupied by the head of the household) or turning her bed so that she is facing the more youthful, playful and creative chi energies of the west, south-east or east.

To surround your daughter in more passive yin energy, decorate her room with cream colours and lacy fabrics. You can also encourage her to wear pastel-coloured clothes, such as pale blue, pink and green. Keeping plenty of plants with large floppy leaves, big soft cushions and lots of soft natural fabrics in her bedroom will also increase the presence of yin energy there. Be sure to reduce the amount of fast-flowing, yang chi energy in her bedroom and play area by covering hard, shiny surfaces with soft rugs or natural fabrics.

For a more long-term approach, encourage your daughter to take up quiet yin hobbies such as reading or drawing. Make her diet a little more yin by preparing meals that contain plenty of vegetables and fruit. Eating less meat, eggs and salty foods will further help.

solution

The thundery chi energy of the east will encourage your children to be more active, alert and adventurous. You should therefore try to generate more of this energy in your home so that it mixes into your children's own personal chi energy fields. Surrounding your children in a more dynamic, yang environment will also make them less inclined to sit around the house being inactive.

To increase the presence of eastern chi energy, place a flowing water feature, such as a small fountain, in the east of your home. You can also place a water feature in the east of your children's bedrooms. Growing tall plants in these areas will further boost the presence of eastern chi energy. Choose bright green bed linen, cushion covers and other fabrics to decorate your children's bedrooms. Since wood is the Five Element related to eastern chi energy, try to place furniture made from solid wood in your children's bedrooms or in the east of your home generally.

Your children will be able to absorb eastern chi energy while they sleep if you turn their beds so that the tops of their heads are pointing in this direction. If this is not possible, turn their beds so their heads point towards the north-east, south-east or south, as these are also generally more active energies.

To create a more yang environment in your children's bedrooms and play areas, keep them clean, tidy and free of clutter. Open spaces, especially at the centre of these rooms, will allow chi energy to move more freely and thus encourage more yang energy. To keep the atmosphere fresh and alive, open the bedroom windows every day so that fresh air can circulate throughout.

You can also encourage your children to become more yang by making sure their diets contain slightly more yang foods, such as grains, vegetables and fish. At the same time, aim to reduce their consumption of the more yin foods, such as ice creams, sweets, soft drinks and other sugary foods.

My children prefer to sit around watching television or playing computer games rather than do anything active. How can I change the atmosphere in our home to prevent them turning into couch potatoes?

problem

things to avoid

Because the chi energies of the south-west or north-east can foster jealous feelings, make sure your toddler's bed is not positioned in such a way that he is sleeping with the top of his head pointing in either of these directions.

solution

Although most children experience feelings of jealousy when they are suddenly no longer the sole recipient of their parents' attention, being surrounded by too much soil chi energy can exacerbate this problem. The chi energies of the south-west, north-east and centre are all associated with soil, so aim to subdue these energies in your home. As well as being associated with soil energy, the south-west can make your child feel more insecure and clingy, north-eastern chi energy can make him compete more for your attention, and the chi energy of the centre can enhance his desire to be your focus of attention.

To reduce the amount of soil chi energy in your home, you will need to activate more metal energy because this has a draining effect on the soil energy. Metal and round-shaped objects – a round metal pot, a silver decorative dish or a metal clock are good examples – kept in the south-west, north-east and centre of your home will help to generate more metal energy. You can also place grey and silver-coloured objects and fabrics in these areas of your home, as well as in your toddler's bedroom, to help boost metal chi energy. Keep the centre of your home and the centre of your child's room as open and free of any furniture as possible to reduce the negative soil chi energy further.

Western chi energy relates to being more content, playful and easy-going, so surrounding your son in more of this energy will help to stem his jealousy. To do this, turn his bed so that he is sleeping with the top of his head pointing in this direction and place tall plants and red flowers in a metal container in the west of his bedroom.

Keeping round, metal objects in the south-west, north-east and centre of your child's bedroom will help to stem his jealousy.

CAREER

5

problem

I'm about to begin looking for work and would like to know if there is anything special I can do to improve my chances of finding a job?

solution

It is better to be slightly more yang when looking for a job because this type of energy encourages you to feel confident and assertive. Potential employers are more likely to view people with yang energy as being alert, decisive and focused. Absorbing more chi energy of the east will also be useful when you start job-hunting because this particular type of energy helps you to feel enthusiastic and positive, making you more inclined to go out and effect change.

To absorb more yang energy, undertake a major spring clean of your home: get rid of belongings you no longer use or need, take down and wash curtains, move heavy furniture so that you can clean behind them and tackle other places that are usually inaccessible. Try to keep your home spacious so that chi energy can flow freely, and open windows regularly to allow in fresh air. Eating more yang foods, such as fish, grains and root vegetables will help you to become more yang, as will taking up a martial art or doing more outdoor sports.

To boost the presence of eastern chi energy in your home, place a bowl of fresh water or another water feature in this direction of your home. Since tree is the Five Element related to the east, place wooden furniture, surfaces or decorative items in the east of your home, and grow tall plants there as well. Decorating this part of your home with bright green colours will further enhance your exposure to this beneficial chi energy.

To absorb more chi energy of the east at night, turn your bed so that the top of your head is pointing towards the east. If this direction is not possible, aim for a south-east direction.

It will be easiest to succeed in finding a new job when your Nine Ki year number is in the east, south-east or south.

EAST

solution

When looking for work as a 'mature-age' person, it would be best to focus on jobs that require mature characteristics, such as wisdom, a broad experience of life and a good understanding of colleagues and customers. To help you to become more employable generally, try to boost your exposure to north-western and south-western chi energy – the chi energy of the north-west will help you to be more organized, take responsibility and act with dignity, while the chi energy of the south-west will encourage you to be caring, considerate, realistic, practical and methodical.

To increase your exposure to north-western chi energy, keep a round metal pendulum clock in the north-west of your home. Since metal is the Five Element related to this direction, silver dishes, metal statues and any other heavy metal objects kept in this part of your home will further enhance north-western chi energy. You can also decorate the north-west of your home with the colours off-white, grey and silver to bring out this energy. Similarly, wear clothes in these colours, along with metal jewellery.

To surround yourself with more south-western chi energy, keep fresh cut yellow flowers in a terracotta vase or fill a clay pot with bits of charcoal and place these in the south-west of your home. Keeping yellow, beige or black fabrics and decorative objects in this part of your home will also help, as will wearing clothes in these colours. You can further enhance your exposure to south-western energy by lighting candles in the south-west of your home.

problem

I have not worked for a long time now, and I'm worried about rejoining the job market. What should I be doing to make myself more attractive to potential employers or more hireable generally?

Absorbing more chi energy of the north-west will help to make you more organized, dignified and responsible, all of which are attractive attributes to a potential employer. To do this, keep round metal objects in the north-west of your home and wear round, metal accessories.

problem

For some time I've been in a rut at work and I'm now considering a career change. What would make me focus better on an alternative career or indicate when the right time to make a move would be?

solution

To be more decisive generally it would help if you absorbed more chi energy of the north-east. This sharp, piercing energy is similar to a cold north-easterly wind, enabling you to clear your mind and spot new opportunities. Enhancing the chi energy of the east is also useful because it encourages enthusiasm, confidence and motivation, all of which are necessary characteristics if you want to change your career.

To add more north-eastern chi energy to your environment, put some white crystal rocks in this part of your home. Decorating this area with stone ornaments, stone surfaces and brilliant white colours will further bring out this energy, as will keeping lit candles and plants with pointed leaves, such as yuccas. You can also try wearing white clothes as these may surround you in more north-eastern energy. To absorb more of this energy at night, turn your bed so that you are sleeping with the top of your head pointing in this direction.

To increase the presence of eastern chi energy in your home and work space, place a water feature, such as a bowl of fresh clean water or an aquarium, in the east of your home or office. Because green is the colour associated with the east, try to decorate the east of your home and office with green fabrics and items, and wear more green clothing. Another suggestion would be to grow tall plants in the east of your home and office. Sitting at your desk so you are facing the east when you work will also enable you to absorb more of this helpful energy. Similarly, sleep with the top of your head pointing in this direction.

The most auspicious times to make this kind of career move are when your Nine Ki year number is in the east, north-east, south-east or north-west.

solution

Success at an interview usually requires confidence, enthusiasm and a clear head. In Feng Shui terms, these feelings are encouraged by the chi energy of the east and south-east. To improve your chances of getting the job you want, you therefore need to increase the presence of eastern or south-eastern chi energy in your home.

One way to do this is to place a small, moving water feature on a waist-high window sill, table or shelf in the east or south-east of your home. Ideally, it should be close to a window so that the eastern or south-eastern sunlight can shine on the water in the mornings. If you do not have a water feature, you can use a small bowl filled daily with fresh, clean water.

To immerse yourself in more eastern or south-eastern energy, turn your bed so that the top of your head points in one of these directions. Try also to sit facing one of these directions when filling in job applications and telephoning prospective employers.

To create more upward-flowing, positive energy in the east or south-east of your home, place fresh flowers or tall plants there. Hanging mirrors in these directions will also do the job, but make sure they are not facing your bed, a door, another mirror or a window. In general, the colour green increases the energy associated with starting something new so, where possible, decorate your home with this colour. A thorough clean out is also a good idea as it will refresh the atmosphere of your home, lift your spirits and help you feel ready to take on new challenges.

The best times to apply for a new job are when your Nine Ki year number is in the east or south-eastern phase.

I have an interview for a new job that is important to me and I would appreciate any advice that will improve my chances of success.

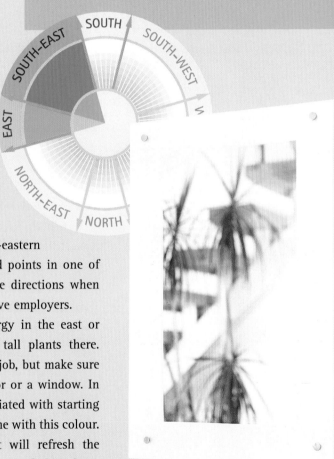

SOUTH-EAST SOUTH SOUTH-WEST EAST NORTH-EAST NORTH

Hanging a mirror in the east or south-east of your home will generate more uplifting and positive chi energy, which is helpful for improving your job prospects.

building materials

In Feng Shui, all building materials can be classified in terms of yin and yang (see below). As a consequence, the materials used to construct your home will influence the flow of chi energy inside it. More yin materials, such as timber and brick, allow chi energy to flow smoothly and gently into a building, bringing its inhabitants closer to the healthy chi generated by the sun, moon and planets. Yang materials, such as granite stone and metal, are rather dense and will therefore make it more difficult for the outside chi energy to pass through walls and floors into your home. Generally, the thicker the walls, the more intense these effects will be.

YIN OR YANG?

If your home has stone surfaces, you will be exposed to more fast-flowing yang chi energy. This is because the hard, smooth texture will speed up the flow of chi energy. Thick external stone walls will also isolate a home from the surrounding environmental chi energy. If you have thick stone walls, you can off-set this by making sure there are lots of skylights and windows in the room as this will allow chi energy to enter your home more easily.

The slightly porous nature of bricks means that a brick home can 'breathe' chi more easily than stone. However, the surface of bricks is quite rough and if internal walls are brick,

Building materials are either yin or yang: natural finished wood, soft wood, polished hard wood (far left), cloth fabrics, dull metal and rush matting tiles are all yin, whereas shiny metal, polished stone, marble, glass and hardwood are yang. Yang materials are often used for commercial buildings, such as the British Airways office in London (immediate left).

this can slow down the flow of chi and lead to a greater risk of stagnation. The solution to this is to plaster internal brick walls, creating a smooth surface that allows a balanced flow of chi energy. Plaster is a material that also allows a home to breathe in healthy chi energy from the outdoor environment.

As wood originates from a living plant, it is considered the most healthy and alive of all materials, encouraging chi to flow through your home. The harder, darker woods, such as mahogany, are more yang, whereas the softer, lighter woods, such as pine, are more yin.

Breeze blocks have become a popular material for modern buildings. Constructed from composites based on cement, they are similar to bricks, but more yang. Breeze blocks have open spaces running through them, which are often filled with synthetic insulating foam. All synthetic materials hinder the flow of chi energy, and the foam in breeze blocks is no different. For this reason, I don't recommend that you use this material in your home.

Glass is a rather unusual surface in that it is very hard, shiny and flat – all yang characteristics – yet it allows chi energy to flow into your home easily in the form of light and radiated heat. Large glass surfaces speed up the flow of chi energy, but you can slow this down by placing plants and fabrics, such as curtains or throws, nearby.

NEIGHBOURHOOD CHI

Most commercial buildings are made of yang materials, while the majority of residential dwellings are constructed from yin materials. It is common to find a lot of buildings in one neighbourhood that have exteriors made from the same type of material, be it wood, brick or glass. In these cases, you will find that there is a particular type of energy permeating the whole neighbourhood. When a building that is built of different materials – a modern steel and glass-fronted office block, for example – exists in a predominantly yin residential neighbourhood, the local inhabitants may be affected by the building and start to feel a little tense, irritable or aggressive. To counter this, introduce more yin materials in and around your home.

Materials can be classified in terms of the Five Elements, enabling you to manipulate chi even further: soil is represented by plaster, china, clay, brick and ceramics; water by glass; tree by wood, wicker and paper; and metal by stainless steel, brass, iron and stone. Plastic generates fire chi but its use is not advisable and the supporting tree chi energy should be used instead.

problem

I've invited some potential clients to my house for dinner. What can I do to impress them and make them feel that I am the right person with whom to do business?

solution

Initial impressions are often the longest lasting, so I suggest you give your home a thorough clean as this is probably the first thing your guests will notice when they come through your front door. A good clean out will make your home look attractive and also refresh the surrounding chi energy and create a more vibrant and stimulating atmosphere.

The next thing to do is to concentrate on the table setting. The type of crockery and colours you choose for your table decorations all affect the way chi energy flows around the table and will therefore influence the atmosphere surrounding your guests. For a business meeting, a slightly more yang atmosphere is suitable because this will encourage clear-headedness and more precise decision making.

To create free-flowing yang energy, make sure there is plenty of space on the table by removing unnecessary items. Add small items with bright yang colours to the table, for example, red flowers, bright yellow napkins or purple place mats. Hanging a convex mirror in the dining room will help to disperse chi energy and add to the yang atmosphere.

The direction you and your guests face when seated at the dining table will expose you to specific types of chi energy that can be helpful to your aims. For example, if you are proposing a business idea or work arrangement, it would help if you faced south or south-east as these directions relate to self-expression and communication respectively. If you want your guests to be more receptive to your ideas, try seating them so they face south-west, west, north-west or north.

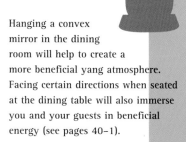

Hanging a convex mirror in the dining room will help to create a more beneficial yang atmosphere. Facing certain directions when seated at the dining table will also immerse you and your guests in beneficial energy (see pages 40–1).

solution

The most helpful energy when negotiating a pay rise is the chi energy of the west. The energy of this direction is associated with the sunset and the harvest, times when people traditionally reflect on their achievements and receive the rewards for all their hard efforts.

The characteristics associated with western chi energy are the colour red, the Five Element metal and round shapes. To increase your exposure to western chi energy, place round, shiny metal coins on a red cloth in the west part of your home or desk. Red flowers in a round metal vase displayed in the west of your home will also bring out this energy. To increase the amount of metal chi energy within your own personal chi energy field, aim to wear red or metal jewellery, jackets with metal buttons or a metal wristwatch. You can also decorate the west of your home with objects and fabrics that are red, pink or grey.

To absorb more western chi energy at night, turn your bed so that the top of your head is pointing towards the west. Similarly, try to face this direction when you are sitting for long periods of time, for example, when you are at work or relaxing at home.

The best time to negotiate an increase in your salary is when your Nine Ki year number is in the west. Other helpful times are when it is in the north-west or south-east.

just common sense

One way to maximize your chances of increasing your salary is to frequently remind yourself of your talents and attributes. As a result, you will be more confident about and feel justified in asking your boss for a pay rise.

WEST

problem

I work for myself and need to win people's respect and confidence to get new contracts. I feel I could do more to achieve this and would like to know what Feng Shui can offer in this respect.

solution

You will find it easier to make an impression and win people's respect if you are slightly more yang, since this energy enables you to project yourself in a more confident manner. You will also find it helpful to immerse yourself in more north-western chi energy. This energy fosters greater wisdom, organizational skills and feelings of being in control. With these attributes it will become easier to develop your leadership potential so that others perceive you as a reliable, responsible and trustworthy person with whom they feel comfortable doing business.

To make yourself more yang, wear brightly-coloured accessories, such as a tie or scarf, and eat more yang foods, such as grains, fish and cooked vegetables. You can also ensure that your home and office are well ventilated and that you frequently spend time outdoors. Taking up regular outdoor exercise will further help you to become more yang.

To absorb more of the beneficial chi energy of the north-west, keep round metal objects, such as round silver plates or a mirror with a round silver frame, in the north-west of your home or office. Try keeping bright red or purple flowers in a metal vase on the north-west part of your desk as this will generate more yang and north-western chi energy simultaneously. Placing a round-faced pendulum clock with as many metal parts as possible in the north-west of your home will help you to develop more structured routines that will make you more dependable. In addition, decorate the north-west of your office with greys and silvers because these colours are associated with north-western energy.

At business meetings arrange the seating plan so that you are sitting in the north-west of the room facing south-east. This will ensure that your clients are facing north-west.

You are most likely to find it easiest to develop confidence and reliability when your Nine Ki year number is in the north-west.

Placing red or round metal objects in the north-west of your home will surround you in more north-western chi energy, which is helpful for developing leadership skills.

problem

I have recently started working from home and would greatly appreciate some Feng Shui advice on how to make this successful.

solution

First of all, you need to set up a proper office space. If you can, avoid working from your bedroom because the more yang chi energy that is required for an office is not compatible with the more yin environment required for good sleep at night.

The ideal directions in which to set up an office are east, south-east, west or north-west from the centre of your home. The chi energy of the east will encourage feelings of confidence and enthusiasm, which are essential when starting and building up a business. The chi energy of the south-east will help you to generate ideas and communicate them effectively and persistently. Western chi energy encourages you to be more goal-oriented and financially aware, and north-western chi energy will help you to command respect and trust from your clients.

Depending on which attribute you feel would help you most, situate your desk in the east, south-east, west or north-west of your office. Facing one of these directions when you work will also help to immerse you in more of that particular energy. Make sure you can see the main door and windows when you are seated at your desk, although this is not as important as getting the direction right.

Endeavour to keep your desk area clean and tidy. Use drawers, filing cabinets and other storage equipment so that everything has its own place. This will reduce the risk of clutter building up and prevent you from feeling confused or disoriented. Try to keep electrical equipment as far away from you as practical as this will reduce your exposure to electromagnetic fields, which can affect your productivity (see also pages 82–3).

dimensions and shapes

When creating a specific atmosphere at home or in the office to resolve problems in your life, you need to bear in mind that the dimensions of a room will affect the flow of chi energy. In general, the larger the room, the more space there is for chi energy to move about and pick up speed easily. This is particularly the case if the room is sparsely furnished. It is therefore easier to create a stimulating and inspiring yang ambience in large, spacious rooms. A smaller room, especially if it is heavily furnished, will slow the flow of chi energy, making it easy to create a cosier and more intimate yin atmosphere there.

The overall shape of a home or office block will also affect the type of energy that flows there. If a building is long and narrow from above, a church for example, it will generate more yin energy. If the building is round, octagonal or square, it is more yang. The Albert Hall is a good example of a round-shaped building that encourages an enthusiastic and stimulating yang atmosphere. A house or apartment that spreads out in many directions tends to encourage slow-moving chi energy, which creates a more yin atmosphere.

SPECIFIC DIMENSIONS

A tall space or room with a high ceiling, such as a cathedral, ballroom or museum, will encourage chi energy to move vertically. This type of movement makes it easier to feel connected to the chi energy of the heavens and earth, which is helpful for feeling mentally stimulated, coming up with original ideas and generally thinking about the bigger issues in life. A wide room or space with low ceilings will encourage chi energy to flow horizontally. This type of movement will help you to feel more connected to things around you, making it easier to feel close to the people you are with. You might find it easier to communicate your feelings and exchange ideas with them. A

I often get my greatest inspiration for book writing in buildings that have high ceilings. This is because the chi energy there moves vertically and is more yang, helping to stimulate the mind and encourage original thought.

restaurant with a low ceiling, for example, will have the right kind of energy for heart-to-heart discussions with a lover.

A square or circular room will cause the chi energy there to be more compact. This type of movement creates more yang energy, which will help you to feel more alert and dynamic. Square or circular rooms are therefore ideal spaces in which to get things done, so consider this shape for your study, office or kitchen. You need to be careful with circular rooms, however, because although the risk of chi energy stagnating in corners is non-existent,

the risk of it spinning around the room increases. This type of chi movement can cause a lack of direction and confusion. Quick changes are also more likely to happen in a circular space, so avoid these if you need greater stability in your life, but seek them out if you want to behave spontaneously.

A long, thin rectangular room or a long, oval-shaped room encourages more yin chi energy. This is particularly the case with oval rooms because the lack of corners means that chi energy flows smoothly. Rectangular rooms spread chi energy in an uneven manner as two or more of the Eight Directions cover the greatest area of the space. For example, a long, thin room with a north-south orientation will have an excess of northern and southern energy, but a deficiency of eastern and western energy. These rooms will have a distinct atmosphere depending on their orientation, which is difficult to rectify even with Feng Shui solutions.

The height of chairs should also be considered. A tall stool or chair aligns you with more rising tree chi energy, which makes it easier for you to feel alert, active and ambitious. Sitting on a low sofa or a large cushion on the floor will expose you to the more settled, soil chi energy, which helps you to feel relaxed and close to others.

A long, thin rectangular room will have more a more yin atmosphere, which is good for encouraging gentle and imaginative feelings.

The shape of a room is hard to alter, but Feng Shui solutions, such as plants, can help to change the flow of chi energy there.

problem

I am concerned that others at work seem to communicate more powerfully than me. They hold the attention of colleagues and clients, their ideas are accepted and they receive acclaim. How can I be more effective in getting my ideas across?

solution

To be effective at communication, it would be helpful to absorb more of the chi energies of the south-east and south: the south-east is particularly good for interacting with others, while the south will enable you to express your thoughts and ideas more powerfully. It would also help to be more yang as this chi energy is good for asserting yourself and gaining confidence in your abilities.

To absorb more south-eastern or southern chi energy when you are at work, make sure you sit facing one of these directions when you are in office meetings. Wearing clothes that have vertical lines, zigzag patterns or speckles of dark green, dark blue and bright purple will also surround you in more south-eastern and southern chi energy.

Aim to keep the south and south-east of your office or workspace clean and tidy. You can also place tall plants or an aquarium with fast-moving fish in the south-east of your desk or office. At home, keep bright lights or lit candles in the south to bring out more southern chi energy. Growing lots of pointy-leaved plants, such as yuccas or palms, in the south of your home will also achieve this.

To surround yourself in more yang energy, make sure your living and workspaces are organized and free of clutter. Hard surfaces, such as stone, glass and marble, and brighter colours, like oranges, reds and purples, will encourage chi energy to move about more quickly, generating more yang energy. Eating a diet rich in fish, grains and root vegetables will help you to become more yang, as will pursuing vigorous outdoor exercise, competitive sports or martial arts.

Placing an aquarium with fast-moving fish in the south-east of your home or plants with spiky leaves in the south of your home will immerse you in the kind of chi energy that will help you to communicate more powerfully.

solution

problem

I've been passed over several times for promotion and feel I'm not getting the recognition I deserve. How can Feng Shui help me become better known for my work?

This predicament suggests a lack of exposure to north-western and southern chi energies. The serious chi energy of the north-west relates to leadership, responsibility and commanding respect, while the fiery, bright chi energy of the south makes it easier for you to express yourself and get noticed.

To increase the amount of north-western chi energy surrounding you, I suggest you place a round-faced pendulum clock with as many metal parts as possible in the north-west of your home or office. Having an off-white, grey or silver-coloured desktop, lamp or filing cabinet will also immerse you in more of this beneficial energy. Similarly, choose these colours when buying a briefcase, work diary, stationery and other office paraphernalia. Wearing a round metal wristwatch, circular metal cufflinks or jewellery will further boost the amount of north-western chi energy to which you are exposed.

To enhance southern chi energy, use bright, direct lighting in the south of your home, or light candles here frequently. Bright purple is the colour associated with the south, so wear accessories in this colour or decorate your office space with purple items and objects. One simple and easy way of introducing purple into your office is by keeping some fresh purple-flowering plants, such as African violets or begonias, on your desk.

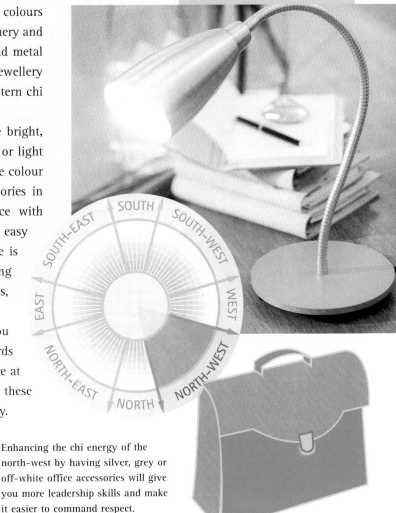

Depending on which direction you think would help you most, sit facing towards either the north-west or south when you are at work. You should also aim to keep both these areas of your desk and office clean and tidy.

You are most likely to be promoted when your Nine Ki year number is in the north-west, south, east or south-east.

Enhancing the chi energy of the north-west by having silver, grey or off-white office accessories will give you more leadership skills and make it easier to command respect.

problem

I am in charge of a small team, but I often find it is easier to do a task myself rather than waste time explaining the job to someone else. How can I learn to delegate to others?

solution

Eastern chi energy is associated with the spring and the sun rising, times when you are more likely to rush about being active and getting things done. Being absorbed in too much of this energy, however, will make you impatient, with the result that you would prefer to do things yourself rather than spend time teaching someone else to do them.

To be better able to delegate, you should aim to reduce your exposure to eastern chi energy and try to expose yourself to more north-western energy. This energy is good for developing leadership skills and viewing goals in the long term, which will encourage you to see the benefits of delegating to others.

Eastern chi energy is associated with tree chi energy, which can be calmed by generating more yin fire energy. Keeping lit candles, pale purple decorative objects and fabrics, and a spider plant in the east of your home or office will therefore help to reduce your exposure to the detrimental energy of the east. You can also turn your bed so that your head is not pointing towards the east at night, and avoid sitting facing this direction when you are at work.

To absorb more north-western chi energy, sleep with the top of your head pointing north-west. At work, move your desk so that you are sitting in the north-west of your office facing south-east. This position will mean that you are exposed to both the leadership qualities of north-western chi energy and the positive communication characteristics of south-eastern chi energy.

Being reluctant to hand work over to others may also be a sign that you are too yang. It would therefore help if you adopted a more yin lifestyle by eating plenty of fruit and vegetables and doing calming, relaxing activities like t'ai chi.

The chi energy of the north-west will encourage you to delegate. You can absorb more of this energy if you move your desk to this direction of your office or workspace.

solution

Being surrounded in too much yang energy can stifle the creative process, so one solution to your problem is to become more yin. This chi energy encourages you to think imaginatively and will help you to generate new ideas. Another Feng Shui remedy to your problem is to absorb more chi energy of the south-east. This energy relates to morning and spring changing to summer, times of rising energy that bring with them growth and freshness. Wind is the symbol of nature associated with the south-east, so absorbing yourself in more of the energy of this direction will help you to spread your ideas the way wind scatters seeds.

To become more yin, change your diet so that you are eating a high proportion of vegetables, salads and fruit. Avoid extremely yang foods such as meat, eggs and salty cheeses. Wear pale-coloured clothes more often and aim to take up gentle, relaxing hobbies. Painting, music and sculpture are all yin hobbies that also help to develop your creativity. Try to break out of fixed routines and do things that are new and different. It may also help to spend more time in buildings that have high ceilings, such as cathedrals and museums.

To increase the amount of south-eastern chi energy in your home, place a water feature, such as a bowl of water, in the south-east of your home. Make sure you refill the bowl with fresh water each morning. Growing tall plants in this part of your home will further boost this energy, as will keeping lots of wooden furniture and decorative objects there. Aim to wear dark green and sky blue clothes and consider these colours when using fabrics or otherwise decorating in the south-east of your home. Display offbeat or unusual works of art in your home and office as this may help to boost your imagination as well.

problem

I seem to lack ideas and the ability to come up with solutions at work. Is there any way I can be more creative and use my imagination more?

Absorbing more yin chi energy will help you to think imaginatively. To do this, take up a creative and relaxing hobby, such as painting, and wear pale-coloured clothes.

problem

I am easily distracted and my moments of poor concentration mean I make silly mistakes at work. I fear this will jeopardize my future with the company. How can Feng Shui help?

solution

In Feng Shui, a lack of concentration is often a sign that you are too yin. Surrounding yourself in more yang energy will therefore help with this problem. Absorbing more south-western chi energy will further help because this chi energy is associated with the afternoon and when summer turns into autumn – times which symbolize an improvement in the quality of nature, rather like fruit ripening on the vine. Increased exposure to south-western chi energy means you will be less inclined to rush into things without thinking and so prevent thoughtless errors. You are also more likely to develop and maintain a high standard of quality at work, which can only improve your career prospects.

To become more yang, wear brightly coloured clothes and eat more wholegrains, root vegetables and fish. Playing an outdoor sport that requires a high degree of concentration, such as tennis, squash or golf, will also help to improve your concentration and make you more yang.

For increased exposure to south-western chi energy, keep a yellow flowering plant in a clay container in the south-west of your home or office. Try to incorporate the colours black, yellow, brown or beige into your living or workspace, be it via furniture, cushions, wall hangings or other decorations. Sleeping with the top of your head pointing south-west will immerse you in more of this chi energy, as will sitting facing this direction at work.

You will find it easiest to concentrate when your Nine Ki year number is in the south-west, north-west or north. When your Nine Ki year number is in the east there is a risk that you will be less patient and make simple mistakes as a result.

Becoming more yang by playing outdoor sports and eating fish and other yang foods is one way to improve your concentration.

solution

Tardiness can sometimes be a problem first thing in the morning, in which case you need to address your ability to wake up at a suitably early time (see page 42). If you have a problem being punctual throughout the day, you will need to immerse yourself in more chi energy of the north-west. This energy strengthens your sense of responsibility and improves your self-discipline and organizational skills. To increase your exposure to north-western chi energy, place a white flowering plant, such as a peace lily, in the north-west of your home or silver, off-white or grey office accessories on the north-west part of your desk at work. Keeping a clock with as many metal parts as possible in the north-west of your bedroom, home or office will also help: metal will help to build up north-western chi energy and a clock will add rhythm and routine to this area. If you don't have a metal clock, a metal statue is a good alternative.

To increase your ability to remember important dates and appointments, reduce your intake of sugar. Sugar is a yin food and, in terms of chi energy, can increase the risk of forgetfulness. Mineral-rich foods, such as miso soup, whitebait and root vegetables can encourage you to be more organized.

To help you be more organized at work, keep your desk tidy and uncluttered. A messy desk makes it harder to feel in control of your life and this, in turn, can discourage punctuality. To make sure your desk is well organized, keep an in/out filing tray and don't allow paperwork to build up on your desk. Anything that you don't need frequent access to should be put away in a desk drawer. To keep track of your appointments, place a diary in a prominent position, preferably in the north-west direction of your desk. Note down every work meeting, deadline or office event you arrange in your diary, and make sure you refer to it frequently throughout the day!

problem

I am often late for work and am disorganized when I get there. I'm never going to progress to a more senior level unless I can correct both these character traits. What could I do to bring this about?

just common sense

Like everything, all these measures will be effective only if you have the desire to be punctual and better organized. You really need to understand the reasons for your undesirable habits if you want to change them.

NORTH-WEST

problem

I find myself becoming increasingly impatient with others at work and, at times, lose my temper. This is spoiling my relationship with my colleagues. How can I calm down?

things to avoid

Make sure your bed isn't positioned so that your head is pointing towards the east when you are asleep. Similarly, avoid facing this direction when you are working at your desk.

solution

In Feng Shui, anger and irritability are emotions that are related to the thundery chi energy of the east. Being too yang will also make you tense and snappy. To improve relations with your colleagues, you should aim to reduce your exposure to eastern chi energy and adopt a more yin lifestyle. Absorbing more south-western or western chi energy will further help because these energies encourage you to be more caring towards and playful with your workmates respectively.

To calm eastern chi energy, light candles in this direction of your home. Decorating the east of your home or office with pale purple colours will further help to calm this detrimental energy.

To boost your exposure to south-western chi energy, buy some fresh cut yellow flowers and place them in a clay container in the south-west of your home or office. To increase western chi energy, choose pink flowers and keep these in a metal container in the west of your home or office. You can also wear more pink and black clothes as these will add more western and south-western energy to your own chi energy field respectively. Try sleeping with the top of your head pointing in one of these directions.

Eating more raw vegetables and fruit, and cutting down on meat, eggs, salt, sugar, coffee, spices and alcohol will make you more yin. As a more long-term measure, your should think about taking up relaxing hobbies, such as yoga, meditation or t'ai chi, because these are excellent ways to channel aggressive feelings.

Placing pink flowers in the west of your home and office will generate more playful, western chi energy, which will help to improve your relationship with your colleagues.

solution

The Feng Shui remedy to this problem would be to set up your office or workspace in a functional manner so that you work productively and can meet your deadlines. At the same time it should have a relaxing ambience to counter your feelings of stress.

To make your office functional, buy filing cabinets and desk trays so that everything has a place and you can find things easily. This will also enable you to keep your office space tidy and your desk surface clear, allowing chi energy to move freely.

To give your office space a more relaxing feel, grow as many plants around you as is practical. This will soften the surrounding chi energy and also help to keep the atmosphere alive, fresh and active. Exposure to EMFs (see pages 82–3) can cause confusion and anxiety, so try to place electrical equipment as far away from you as possible. To encourage a more harmonious flow of chi energy, surround yourself with furniture made from natural materials. Solid wood, metal and pure cotton fabrics are preferable to MDF, plastics or synthetic fibres.

The direction you face when you are sitting at your desk will expose you to different energies that can benefit you in different ways. For example, facing north-west will encourage you to feel more in control of your work. Facing south-east will make it easier to progress smoothly without stress and facing south-west will help you to be more methodical and practical in your work. Choose the direction which you think will benefit you most, or try one direction for a while and then another. Avoid facing towards the south because this could make you feel more stressed, and avoid facing west or north because these might deplete your drive to meet your deadlines. Always aim to sit so that you are facing into a room with a clear sight of the main door as this will make you feel more secure and powerful.

problem

I am often faced with very short and exacting deadlines at work which are proving to be stressful. How can I reduce this stress?

problem

My relationship with my boss seems to be deteriorating. We seem to irritate each other and this is obviously affecting my work. Is there a Feng Shui remedy to this dilemma?

solution

One reason for this problem may be that you or your boss is sitting in an area of the office where the chi energy is moving too fast. This type of energy flow can make you feel irritable, unsettled and tense, and commonly occurs if there are sharp or protruding corners pointing towards your desk. It can also result if a corner of another building is pointing in your direction or your desk is situated at the end of a long corridor or walkway.

To slow the flow of chi energy caused by sharp protrusions, place bushy plants in front of them. Draping fabric over the corners of filing cabinets and desks will have a softening effect. Alternatively, you can avoid this situation by simply choosing furniture with rounded edges.

When the corner of another building is pointing towards you and causing chi energy to move too quickly, you should aim for a more long-term approach by growing bushes, trees or other types of vegetation between your building and the offending corner. Where this is not possible, or as an additional measure, you can deflect the offending chi energy by attaching convex mirrors, a metal plaque or other shiny reflective surfaces onto the outside wall of your building that faces the corner.

To break up the fast flow of chi energy along a corridor, hang mirrors on the walls. Mirrors facing each other cause chi energy to bounce back and forth quickly, so stagger their positions slightly to avoid this, and put a bushy plant opposite each mirror.

If you and your boss work in the same room, arrange your desks so that you face each other at an angle instead of head on, and make sure you can both see the door when seated. You can also put a bushy plant between your desks for extra measure. I suggest you turn your desk so you face south-west, west, north-west or south-east as this will surround you in more peaceful and screne energy.

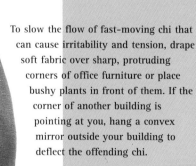

To slow the flow of fast-moving chi that can cause irritability and tension, drape soft fabric over sharp, protruding corners of office furniture or place bushy plants in front of them. If the corner of another building is pointing at you, hang a convex mirror outside your building to deflect the offending chi.

solution

Becoming more yang will help you to acknowledge your true feelings and be less afraid of or intimidated by others. You will also find it useful to absorb more of the thundery chi energy of the east because this energy fosters confidence and therefore helps you to assert yourself.

To increase the presence of eastern chi energy, place a water feature, several tall plants and wooden furniture and objects in the east of your home or office. You can also decorate this area with bright green fabrics and vertical stripes. Wearing clothes of this colour and striped patterns will further surround you in eastern chi energy. To absorb more of this energy at night, turn your bed so the top of your head is pointing eastwards. If this is not possible, aim for the north-west or north-east as these directions help you to command greater respect and to stand up for yourself respectively.

problem

If my boss or colleagues ask me for a favour, I tend to say yes because I like to avoid confrontation. Yet I usually end up resenting this afterwards. What can I do to become more assertive?

To surround yourself in more yang energy, adopt a more yang diet. This can be achieved by increasing your consumption of fish, wholegrains and root vegetables, and generally eating lots of hot meals, such as soups, stews and stir-fries. Avoid eating too many cold meals or sugary foods as these can make you feel more yin and meek.

To make your home more yang, give it a good spring clean and throw out any unwanted or unused items. Try to keep rooms spacious and surfaces clear because this will help chi to move quickly and freely. Adding bright colours to your home will also generate yang energy.

problem

I have been in the same job for many years and I'm finding it increasingly difficult to maintain enthusiasm for my work. I lack motivation and tend to drift through the day. How can I use Feng Shui to improve this situation?

solution

Lacking motivation is a sign that you are too yin. It would therefore help if you adopted a more yang lifestyle. Immersing yourself in the piercing chi energy of the north-east will also help to motivate you because this energy encourages you to spot new opportunities and pursue them vigorously. The chi energy of the east encourages confidence, enthusiasm and a positive outlook, so I would suggest increasing your exposure to this as well.

To make your office more yang, keep the area tidy so there is plenty of space for chi energy to flow smoothly. Organize your desk well and keep it clear of clutter. Add a few brightly coloured items to your work area, such as a red notepad or an orange paperweight as these colours will generate more yang energy. Try to do more outdoor sports and eat more yang foods, such as warm dishes made with grains, fish and vegetables.

As mountains are the symbol of nature related to the north-east, putting white stones or rocks in this part of your home and office will bring out more of this energy. Choose bright white fabrics and household objects to decorate this area as well. The soil energy related to the north-east is supported by fire energy, so you can further boost north-eastern chi energy by placing lit candles in this direction.

To increase your exposure to eastern chi energy, put a small fountain or another moving water feature in this direction of your home or office. Green is the colour associated with the east, so grow tall plants or place other green objects in this part of your home. Wooden furniture and surfaces will also bring out more chi energy of the east.

It will be easiest to be motivated and enthusiastic about your work when your Nine Ki year number is in the north-east or east.

Wearing bright white clothing will immerse you in more chi energy of the north-east, which helps you to feel more enthusiastic and motivated about work.

solution

Unfortunately, office politics are often a fact of life. Although you may not be able to prevent them, you can limit the negative and unsettling impact they have on you. To achieve this, develop greater independence and learn to detach yourself from whatever is going on around you. Ideally, you should be perceived by others as someone who can rise above all this. Bear in mind, too, that the more confident you are about yourself, the less you will be affected.

To become more independent and objective, immerse yourself in northern chi energy. This energy is associated with water energy, which enables you to flow around and avoid other people's problems more easily. To expose yourself to more water energy, turn your desk so you are facing north. Keep cream flowers on your desk as these generate more calming energy. Being more independent and objective will be easiest to achieve when your Nine Ki year number is in the north.

If you have an authoritative manner and command the respect of your colleagues, people are less likely to engage you in their petty jealousies and gossip. To enhance your responsible image, sit in a position where you are facing north-west. A more formal appearance will also help. North-west is also associated with metal energy, so try to keep objects made of metal, such as a lamp or paperweight, nearby. Try wearing metal accessories such as a large watch or jewellery. The colours off-white, light grey and silver also increase north-western chi energy, so wear clothes in these colours or decorate your desk and immediate surroundings with objects in these colours. When your Nine Ki year number is in the north-west it will be easiest to achieve greater dignity and command respect.

Eastern chi energy can make you feel more confident and may help to increase your self-esteem, allowing you to rise above petty issues and not feel unsettled by gossip. To absorb more of this energy, sit in an east-facing position. Keeping plenty of plants and bright green objects around you will further help.

You will feel most confident when your Nine Ki year number is in the east. It will be more difficult to avoid office politics when your Nine Ki year number is in the south or south-west.

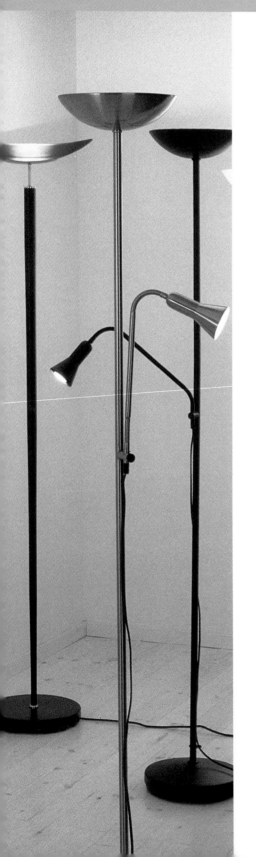

lighting

Lights generate fiery yang chi energy, so having lots of lighting in a room will make the atmosphere more dynamic and exciting. Because light waves also help to activate the existing chi energy of a space, lighting is especially useful to have in areas that risk harbouring stagnating chi energy, for example in a basement flat or office, in the corners of a room, below heavy beams and in rooms with low or sloping ceilings. Lights placed in the south of a room or home will strengthen the Five Element fire chi energy. When kept in the south-west, north-east or centre of a space, they will nourish the Five Element soil chi energy, which is supported by fire chi energy.

Ideally, buildings should be designed with large windows and skylights to allow as much natural light into the area as possible. This way, artificial lighting would be needed only in the evenings or when the weather is overcast.

LIGHTS FOR DIFFERENT OCCASIONS

Electric lights come in all different types and styles, and the following information will give you a better idea of which ones are best suited to creating specific types of environments.

Incandescent light bulbs emit a broad angle of uniform light, so are good for general household lighting. They increase the chi energy over a wide area in a relatively even manner. The colour of incandescent lighting is slightly orange, a colour of light that helps to create a warm and more yin atmosphere.

Spotlights allow you to focus the light in a particular place, which is good for activating chi energy in certain parts of your home – a decorative feature on the wall, a desk or a kitchen table – while allowing the rest of the room to remain in natural light.

Up-lights, spotlights and other standing lamps are easy Feng Shui tools to incorporate into your home. As well as the atmosphere each type of light helps to create, bear in mind the colour and material of the stand, as these also have an effect on chi.

Low-voltage halogen lights produce a high-intensity light that is ideal for increasing the flow of chi energy through stagnant areas. These lights are more compact than most other types and are therefore easily recessed into ceilings. They are also small enough to be used in free-standing lamps that can create up or down-lighting.

Up-lights encourage a more upward flow of chi energy. This is particularly helpful if you have a low or sloping ceiling. If you direct the lighting onto the ceiling, it will make the ceiling seem higher than it actually is. Lights reflected onto walls will diffuse and spread the light, which creates a more yin atmosphere. The lighter the colour of the wall surface, the greater the reflection.

Table lamps or lamps placed on the floor will make a room feel cosy and intimate. Lampshades made from fabric or paper will create a more yin atmosphere, whereas metal or reflective lampshades generate more yang energy, which is less relaxing.

Fluorescent lights produce a colder, blue hue of light that can create a harsher, yang atmosphere. In addition, fluorescent lights radiate more intense electromagnetic radiation, which can increase the incidence of headaches and mental fatigue. I would therefore avoid having these lights in your home.

Soft, indirect lighting generates more yin chi energy. You should therefore use this type of lighting – be it candles or lampshades – if you want to create a more intimate, gentle or romantic kind of atmosphere in a room.

CANDLE LIGHTS

Candles are the most yin form of lighting because they emit a softer, orange light and do not generate any electromagnetic radiation. Try to use candles when you want to create a softer, more romantic atmosphere in your bedroom, living room, dining room or even your bathroom.

The colour of the candles you choose will also have a significant effect on the chi energy it generates, so you should consider this as well. For example, red or pink candles are good if you want to create a romantic ambience in a room and cream is a good colour if you want to create a calm and tranquil atmosphere. For more information on colours, see pages 114–15.

problem

I am rapidly approaching retirement age and gradually would like to scale down my work load and commitments. What is the best way of doing this?

solution

Absorbing more chi energy of the west is useful when preparing for retirement because this energy is associated with the harvest and sunsets, times that symbolize the completion of life cycles. Western chi energy will foster financial security and feelings of contentment about your new life. The chi energy of the north-west is also beneficial because it relates to wisdom, helping you to feel in control of the transition from working to retirement. It is a particularly useful energy if you plan to consult on a part-time basis.

To absorb more western chi energy, turn your bed so that you are sleeping with the top of your head pointing westward. This is also a good direction to face when you are relaxing at home. Keeping pink flowers in a metal vase, metal coins on a red cloth or silver decorative plates in the west of your home will also increase the presence of this chi energy.

Round, heavy metal objects and silver or grey fabrics will help to build up north-western chi energy, so try to incorporate these shapes and colours into the north-west direction of your home as much as possible. Keeping a round-faced metal pendulum clock in this direction of your home is one way of doing this.

It would also help to make the transition from a more active yang working environment to a more relaxing yin home environment by becoming a little more yin yourself. This will allow you to enjoy the benefits of retirement to the maximum. Try to decorate your home with soft textures and pale-coloured fabrics to create a more peaceful environment. Consider taking up a yin hobby, such as painting, gardening or walking. A more yin diet filled with fresh fruit and vegetables will also help.

The most auspicious time to retire is when your Nine Ki year number is in the west or north-west.

index

acknowledgements

Author acknowledgements:

As this book was written on my laptop in so many different locations during 1999, I would like to thank all those people who made it possible for me to enjoy writing in such inspiring atmospheres.

First of all Dragana, the girl I share my life with and who has created the most beautiful home; my mother, Patsy, whose 14th-century cottage is my sanctuary; Richard and Katy Vernon and Richard Rudland, who have made our holidays in Wales so enjoyable; Lorenzo Poccianti, whose stunning castle in Italy would inspire anyone; Karin Sotirovic, whose home in Monaco has such a warm welcome and fabulous views; Dusica and Enno, whose cosy chalet in Klosters has been our winter refreshment; Boy George, whose gothic mansion has such a grand and inspiring atmosphere; Mary Pisani, who generously provided us with rooms in her spectacular hotels in Malta and arranged for the use of yachts through Trader Marine; Monique Guion from Napoléon's Refuge, which has breathtaking mountain scenery near Briançon in France; and Madame Mellot in Sancerre, Charlotte in Munich, and Daniela Giannandrea in Rome.

Finally, I would like to thank Amy Carroll and Denise Brown, who have always encouraged my book ideas. I would also like to thank the very talented staff at Carroll & Brown, in particular Madeleine Jennings, my editor, and Sandra Brooke, the designer and illustrator of this stylish book.

Carroll & Brown would like to thank:
Elisa Merino, Paul Stradling, Karol Davies, Clair Reynolds, Richard Soar, Dawn Henderson. We would also like to show our appreciation to everyone who lent us props, including Mysteries Arts Ltd, Neal Street East, Wild at Heart and RTW Products.

Picture Credits:
Front cover (left) The Stock Market; (centre right) & 142 (top) Max Gibbs, Oxford Scientific Films Photo Library; 5 (top) & 43 (right) Telegraph Colour Library; (middle) & 86 Pictor International; (2nd bottom) & 101 Tim Street-Porter/Elizabeth Whiting Associates; (bottom) & 143 Ocean Home Shopping Ltd; 7 (2nd bottom) & 64 (top) & 99 (top) Max Gibbs, Oxford Scientific Films Photo Library; 12 (right) RTW Products; 16 G. Hadjo, CNRI/Science Photo Library; 17 (top) Di Lewis/Elizabeth Whiting Associates; 18 & 55 & 149 (background) IKEA; 19 & 31 (bottom) Ocean Home Shopping Ltd; 28 (top) Tom Leighton/Elizabeth Whiting Associates; 33 (right) Mark Luscombe-Whyte/Elizabeth Whiting Associates; 37 Telegraph Colour Library; 45 (left) & 49 Max Gibbs, Oxford Scientific Films Photo Library; 48 The Image Bank; 50 (left) Rodney Hyett/Elizabeth Whiting Associates; (right) & 154 IKEA; 55 Telegraph Colour Library; 68 (left) The Image Bank; 71 (top) Michael Dunne/Elizabeth Whiting Associates; 76 & 130 RTW Products; 77 (bottom) Max Gibbs, Oxford Scientific Films Photo Library; 82 (top) Pictor International; (bottom) IKEA; 83 (top) British Airways/Waterside Development; 86 Pictor International; 88 Telegraph Colour Library; 95 & 112 (right) Ocean Home Shopping Ltd; 96 Dennis Stone/Elizabeth Whiting Associates; 110 (bottom) Tom Leighton/Elizabeth Whiting Associates; 115 Ian Parry/Elizabeth Whiting Associates; 120 (bottom) Tony Stone Images; 125 Elizabeth Whiting Associates; 129 (left) & 139 (right) Tony Stone Images; (right) & 151 Rodney Hyett/Elizabeth Whiting Associates; 133 Ocean Home Shopping Ltd; 134 (top) Jules Selmes; (bottom) British Airways/Waterside Development; 135 (top 3) Jules Selmes; (bottom) British Airways/Waterside Development; 136 Mark Luscombe-Whyte/Elizabeth Whiting Associates; 141 (top) Telegraph Colour Library; (bottom) Jerry Tubby/Elizabeth Whiting Associates; 142 (top) Max Gibbs, Oxford Scientific Films Photo Library; 155 (bottom) Brian Harrison/Elizabeth Whiting Associates.

about the author

Simon Brown began his career as a design engineer and has had two inventions patented in his name. In 1981 he began studies in Oriental medicine and qualified as a shiatsu therapist and macrobiotic consultant. In addition to these healing arts, he studied Feng Shui. For seven years he was director of London's Community Health Foundation, a charity that ran a wide range of courses in Japanese and Chinese healing arts. During this time Simon organized some of the first courses on Feng Shui available to the UK general public. Simon has since made Feng Shui his full-time career. His client list ranges from large public companies (such as British Airways and The Body Shop) to celebrities (including Boy George). Presently, he writes regular features for the magazine *Feng Shui for Modern Living* and conducts training workshops in Lisbon, Munich, Paris, Rome and various cities throughout the UK and US.

All books by Simon Brown use the Japanese compass style of Feng Shui.

Also published by Ward Lock:
Practical Feng Shui
A complete do-it-yourself practical guide to Feng Shui. Explains how Feng Shui works with full colour photographs and drawings. This provides information on how to carry out a Feng Shui survey and offers design solutions for your home. It advises on how to make the most of the shape and location of your home, how best to tackle unusual areas such as utility and storage rooms, staircases, doors and fireplaces, and helps you to understand the effects of sunlight. It also includes information on Feng Shui astrology, based on the Nine Ki system.

Practical Feng Shui for Business
Ideal for anyone who wants to apply Feng Shui to their career, this book explains how to be more successful at work. Full of colourful drawings and photographs to help you to implement Feng Shui in real life situations, the book also includes successful strategies for offices, shops and restaurants.

Practical Feng Shui Astrology
Using the Nine Ki system, learn how to make and read your own birth chart, which can then be used to gain interesting insights into your relationship with lovers, friends and family. This book helps you to work out the best time to make important changes in your life. Also in full colour with quick reference charts that make it fun and easy to use.

Essential Feng Shui
The ideal introduction to Feng Shui, this is a compact edition of *Practical Feng Shui* and contains everything you need to know to create a supportive and harmonious home environment.

Other publications by Simon Brown include: *The Principles of Feng Shui* (Thorsons ISBN 0 7225 3347 0), which is now also available as an audio cassette, and *Feng Shui Food* (Thorsons ISBN 0 7225 3934 7).

For information on Feng Shui consultations and courses with Simon Brown, contact:
PO Box 10453, London NW3 4WD, England.
Tel/fax: 00 44 (0)20 7431 9897.
E-mail: simonbrown_fengshui@compuserve.com.
Visit his website, which includes software for floorplans, on: HTTP://ourworld.compuserve.com/homepages/simonbrown_fengshui.